The Language of the Angels

Claire Nahmad

Souvenir Press

First published in Great Britain in 2012 by Souvenir Press Ltd
43 Great Russell Street, London WC1B 3PD

ISBN 9780285641167

Typeset by Regent Typesetting, London

Printed and bound in Great Britain by
CPI Group (UK) Ltd, Croydon, CR0 4YY

Love and the Maiden, 1877 (tempera with gold paint & gold leaf on canvas), by John Roddam Spencer Stanhope (1829–1908). Private Collection/Photo © Christie's Images/The Bridgeman Art Library

Dedication

This book is dedicated to Eddie and Beryl Nahmad,
with fond memories

Contents

How to use this book

The language of the angels has been known throughout the ages as the Green Language or the Language of the Birds. It was a secret language that only the elect understood. From it derived the Mother Tongue, a global language of signs and symbols and a certain magical essence within words themselves that was shared in secrecy by the Templars, the Masons, the alchemists and many other esoteric groups.

For the purpose of this book I have drawn from the language of the angels in its simplest rendition so that it can be used by anyone and everyone. The language of the angels as it is presented here resides in their names, and in the chanting of their names. In each magical name lives the concept of the angel, providing a vessel for its being in the ethereal worlds. It is this that we can call on to summon the angel to our aid and to facilitate the absorption of its benign influences into our soul.

The names of angels of supernal light and blessing that appear in the following pages have been derived from the oldest texts originating in ancient Mesopotamia, Egypt, India, Persia and Palestine. These names in many cases are linked with the Enochian system of angelic language or with the direct visions of other ancient mystics in which they were revealed. The Enochian system incorporated an alphabet and angelic scripts, for according to ancient texts, the patriarch Enoch, in the days of earliest antiquity, was entrusted with the language of the angels.

Enoch was the son of Cain and Luluwa, both spoken of in ancient Sumerian texts (the oldest in the world and much earlier in origin than those of the Old Testament) as great royal leaders loved by their people. Enoch was a mystic and a visionary and also a great scientist.

His writings in the Book of Enoch, for instance, reveal the first exposition of the 'polar wobble', denoting the fact that the Earth had shifted slightly off its axis. It was Enoch's lifetime's work to transcribe the speech of the angels into sounds that resonated with human hearing and understanding. In several of the ancient manuscripts that were excluded from the Old Testament, it is reported that Enoch nearly met his death many times whilst he performed this almighty feat, because he attuned himself to angelic utterances that, in their cosmic grandeur, atomise frail human consciousness. The angels themselves came to the rescue and prevented Enoch's psyche from exploding into 'flashing silver fragments more numerous than the stars' as he undertook his mighty mission.

When Enoch finally produced his *magnum opus*, it was found to consist of a series of sounds that correlated to birdsong. It was generally agreed that he had indeed delivered the Language of the Angels to humanity. His wondrous lexicon was transcribed further into sigils and symbols, and fitted into concepts of human language. Yet in its original state of pristine grace, this language was actually 'the Language of the Angels'.

The descriptions given of the angels simply depict how they have appeared to mystics of the past, and also how they have appeared to me. They are given to help you to unfold the wings of your imagination and begin to trust in its considerable power. The illustrations were chosen for a similar purpose, in the hope that the sublime angel visions of the masters will stimulate your own inner eye. Even if you think you are not very imaginative, there is no doubt that this power does indeed reside within you. If you see the angels differently from their portrayals, you will be seeing a facet of divine truth. In the higher realms, reality is not the hidebound entity of everyday earthly experience!

There are four simple steps to using this book:

1. The first is to summon the power of your imagination gently and easily so that you can draw close to the angels.
2. The second is to hold a very clear idea in your mind of the service you are asking of the particular angel you have decided to call on.
3. The third is to render that clear idea into a brief and straight-forward request for help from the angel, which can be spoken aloud or silently.
4. The fourth is to chant the name of the angel for a few minutes or perhaps only for a moment or two, according to what feels right for you, whilst continuing to retain the clarified request in your mind.

You will need to carry out these steps one after the other, without any intervening delays. Of course, if you are in an emergency angels can be summoned instantaneously just through calling on them by name or the quality or virtue over which they preside (the Angel of Protection or the Angels of Mercy, for instance). There is no need to work through the four steps under such circumstances. However, working with angels is in the main a gentle and incremental path, and the simple process outlined above is an effective way to initiate communion with them.

The hyphens within the given angelic names are there only to indicate a suggested rhythm for chanting, and do not necessarily signify that the names are formally separated into different syllables. Have no qualms regarding pronunciation, as the angels will always understand you!

We cannot, of course, call on the angels as if communion with them was an 'app' on a mobile phone! It is necessary to still the mind, to have a soft awareness of the rise and fall of the breath, to stimulate the inner eye and to stir the soul in our approach to them. This happens naturally throughout the course of the four steps.

It is helpful to bear in mind that the breath is sacred, and that angels enter into us through its agency. Breathing calmly and rhythmically will help you to see the forms and colours of the angels, to hear their music, to sense their fragrance and to taste the essence of their wisdom and healing. This mysterious current of the breath lifts the vessel of the soul and the imagination into full flight. It seems to be an ordinary and mundane procedure, and of course it is if we only ever use it in everyday mode. Yet it has silver sails, and becomes a flow of miracles, if we will allow it to assume its transformational power.

As you speak the language of the angels, let your chanting be resonant and rhythmical so that it moves in an easy, circular flow. It is worth remembering that it is a language of heavenly magic, of secret wonders and sublime mystery. Speak it with reverence, because the earthly mind will try to steal away its enchantment and potency. Yet, as you enter ever more deeply into the presence of angels through regular communion and receive their many blessings, you will find that the materialistic perspective loses its dominion and can no longer imprison you, because you are in the arms of angels.

Cupid and Psyche, (oil on canvas), by Sir Edward Coley Burne-Jones (1833–98). Sheffield Galleries and Museums Trust, UK/Photo © Museums Sheffield/The Bridgeman Art Library

Angel Healer of Addictions and Obsessions
Ba-glis

Her mode is usually feminine; she is the angel of temperance; her robes are sunlit indigo, creating a most holy blue, with shades of deep lavender dreaming at their verges; her eyes are of vivid silver, unusual and arresting but softly compassionate; her music is the impression of an ethereal guitar and harp with an echo of lutes, keening, sweet and heart-piercing; her perfume is lavender and wild iris.

She restores emotional balance and tenderly resurrects and heals a fractured will and fragmented wisdom. She teaches us to use our will with gentle, relaxed persistence rather than aiming to employ it as a battering ram, from which ill-advised exercise we often fall back, exhausted, undermined and helpless. A deep, quiet, secure centredness, resting tranquilly in the power of the will, is what she teaches, rather than thinking of its potency as something that oppresses and demands. Let her silver eyes gaze into the fathoms of your obsession or addiction and dissolve the tentacles with which it holds you fast. Chant her name and allow her to bring you healing.

Angel of Ancestry
Re-ha-el

His mode is usually masculine; he is a tall, imposing angel, exuding dignity, expansion and continuity; he is known as Son of the Flame and fosters respect for parents and for wisdom arising from ancient sources, not only human but from all the world of Nature and her many kingdoms. Our secret tribal brethren who keep alive certain strands of vital primal knowledge are protected by Rehael. He also presides over health and longevity.

His robes are Madonna blue with touches of the redness of red earth; his music is of slow, mighty grandeur; his perfume is of mountain flowers.

When you are feeling disconnected from your source, when children have no respect for their parents or adults have no respect for the culture that nurtured them, call in this angel as troubleshooter. Rehael will open up the sources of ancestral wisdom within their deeper being and help to resolve the problem. You can also pray to Rehael for preserved health and long life.

Angel Healer of Anger and Antagonism
Col-um-ba

His mode is masculine; on assumption into heaven, it is said that Saint Columba, 'Columcille of the Isles' as Brigid in human guise was 'Bride of the Isles', took on the form of an angel. Compassionate and generous, with a special tenderness for the sufferings of women, whose travail in childbirth he saw as at least on a level with the warrior in the field, Columba forged himself anew on the holy isle of Iona, whence he had travelled from Ireland. A prince and chieftain in his own country, he had been passionate in war and had slain many before he turned to the spiritual life.

He was known as 'wolf' in his early days, but his transformation earned him the title of 'dove' – 'Columba'.

The spirit of Columba will touch you with grace, healing and blessing if you need to transform your own wolves into doves, and forge passion into peace.

Angel of Apples
Il-an-i-el

Her mode is usually feminine; her name carries its own poetry, as if drawn from Tolkien's Elven language; it is Ilaniel who, it is said, often stamps the heart of the apple with a five-pointed star, the sigil of Mother Earth and of the fifth dimensional world into which the Divine Feminine is calling us; she works with the Angel of the Rose, for the apple tree and the rose tree are of the same family, and their sisterhood is sacred. Her fragrant robes are the colours of rose and apple-green; her music is the music of Divine Mother, sweetly soulful yet with a broad fundamental gravitas in its poignancy. Her perfume is that of the apple freshly plucked from the tree, cut open and bitten into.

Call on Ilaniel whenever you eat an apple! Just give her a moment's thought. She will bless the fruit so that it brings you increased goodness, and, if you eat it in meditative mode, she will reveal to you the profound secrets and wisdom of the apple, of the place you fill in Mother Earth's heart and how this and the mystery of the apple connect both you and the Earth to the Ultimate Being, the highest of the high.

Angel of Aquatic Animals
Man-a-kel

His mode is usually masculine; he is a tall angel, giving the impression of monumental power and strength tempered and made beautiful by wisdom; the poet and mystic Fiona Macleod saw him once in startling vision, composed of seawater of an enchantingly beautiful jade green; every muscle, limb and sinew, every facial feature, his long, curling locks of hair, were sculpted to heart-piercing perfection by the configurations of the jade water. He told her that we are children of water, that all creation was brought forth from the mystical tears shed from God's heart that formed primal matter. He is particularly connected with the lifestream of whales, of the 'Cetacean nation', although he protects all marine animals and is linked with a special bond to humanity itself. The Isle of Man is named after him, for he was its god when mortals first settled there. His music is a very beautiful and melodious sighing and rolling, crashing and roaring, which seems a contradiction in terms unless you listen deeply to the music of the sea. Within the dimensions of this music is the song of the whales with its rapturous sonic cries. His perfume is difficult to liken to any fragrance of earth, but it is one of utter renewal and awakening; it stimulates the mind and the spirit in one great unifying surge, as if you were lifted into new liberating ethers on a whale-spout!

Call on Manakel to help and heal the creatures of the sea, and to aid in communicating to the powers that be that they must not plunder and rape the oceans and their inhabitants. Send your love to the whale and the dolphin pods through Manakel, for they will joyfully respond. You can ask him to reveal to you the mysteries that dwell enshrined within him concerning our deepest origins and the secret of our true home.

Angel of the Balances
Dok-i-el

His mode is usually masculine; he is 'the weighing angel', the 'archangel who is like the sun, holding the balance in his hand'; his robes emit golden grandeur; his eyes are penetrating; his music sounds in muted booms and soft roars like the plunge of cataracts; his perfume is benzoin.

Call on Dokiel when you have been thrown off kilter by shock, distress or anger and need a stern, calming hand to deliver checks and balances. Whenever you feel that your life is out of balance, if you wonder whether you are judging a situation appropriately, or you just generally feel 'all over the place', Dokiel will help.

Angel of Beneficence
Tet-ra

Her mode is usually feminine; she grants wishes, although she must not be called upon with selfish or trivial intent; she is spoken of as a 'great and glorious spirit'; her robes are like the Northern Lights, dancing with vivid green, crimson, rose, blue, white, silver and violet; her eyes glow with love and kindliness for her mortal charges; her music is the sound of warm, tender, poignantly melodious violins; her perfume is sweet violets with an elusive undercurrent of rose.

Tetra grants wishes, but note that it is wise to take care that they are not selfish, short-sighted or trivial. This does not mean that you should not ask for little things, such as fair weather for an event. Tetra delights in the granting of humble wishes. An example of a trivial wish might be that we ask for someone else to do our chores because of sheer reluctance to carry them out! (It would be a different matter if we asked because of illness or crisis.) It is also important to make your requests with commitment. For instance, if you asked for an opportunity to learn to play the piano, you would need to be prepared to undergo the necessary labour required in learning the skill, or Tetra would not respond.

In short, she will never indulge your lower nature or grant wishes that waste her energy or importune or inconvenience others. If you find that your wish has not been granted, trust Tetra's wisdom.

Angel of Benevolent Outcomes
Ach-Sah

Her mode is usually feminine; her robes are a glorious flower-yellow, the colour of happiness and buttercups in the grass; she is a sparkling, smiling angel, full of laughter, who expands our narrow judgements with kindly humour and helps us swiftly to retrieve our sense of perspective. Our horizons widen, our perceptual limitations recede, when Ach-Sah draws near. She blesses the dynamics of human relationships, predicaments, situations and scenarios so that all is resolved into a benevolent outcome, and allows us to be generous to ourselves. In Solomonic rites she was called 'the spirit of benevolence'. Her music is the sound of timbrels and clapping hands; her perfume is the scent of flowers carried in the wind.

Call on her whenever you feel you may need help to ensure a benevolent outcome. Ach-Sah will grant it, even if occasionally the package may at first seem strange or disappointing. Give her your trust; then her service to you can blossom. You can enter into a beautiful breathing meditation when invoking Ach-Sah. Simply breathe in when sounding the first syllable of her name and breath out on the last, so that your in-breath is 'Ach' and your sighing exhalation is 'Sah'. Her grace will enter into you through your breath to bring you perfect relaxation and make you feel good.

Angel Protector of Birds of the Wilderness
Trgiaob (Trr-gia-ob)

His mode is usually masculine; he is bright-eyed and soft-plum-aged, like a golden-white bird; he sometimes appears as a winged head, like a cherub, and sometimes as a golden child or an elfin being, although he is angelic in nature; his music is the rhythm of whirrs, clicks, drumming, whistling and purring within birdsong; his perfume is that of flowering meadows

The name of this angel is pronounced rather like a birdcall. Try to get that fluting, chirruping rhythm with which birds sing when you sound his name, and repeat it just as birds delight in the repetitive tempo of their song (the final syllable 'ob' rises pertly in tone). You can summon Trgiaob to protect all wild birds from disease, abuse, reduction in numbers, pollution and the destruction of their habitat, and to heal individual wild birds. You can also invoke him to help you to make friends with the wild birds you encounter on walks or in your garden.

Angel of Birdsong
An-pi-el

Her mode is usually feminine; she has charge of bird life and the magic in birdsong. An abbot that established a monkish com-munity in early medieval times encountered Anpiel, who sang to him from a woodland branch in the form of a white bird. Transfixed, he listened to her rapturous song, then went on his way to carry home brushwood to the humble wattle and daub monastery that the brothers had built. Yet, when he came out of the wood, he found a great abbey built of stone. When he told the strange monks who approached him who he was, they fell on their knees in reverence, exclaiming that he had returned to the order he had founded hundreds of years ago, and that history recorded he had wandered away into the wood one spring morning and mysteriously vanished. Such is the mystic power and spiritual enchantment of Anpiel. Her robes sigh with the shades of evening and enshrine the white fire within the twilight which is the secret of the night reflected in the stars: the beautiful, pure and blessed darkness as lovely as light; her garments also hold the first morning fires and the radiant stars of dawn, for this angel weaves the majesty of the goodly darkness and light into the transcendence of birdsong. Her music is its miracle; her perfume is the mirror of bliss in all its sweet stealing scents.

It has been said of birdsong that if it occurred for only a single day in a certain cycle of years, we would stop our work and play and all our noise to stand and listen to its immeasurable wonder. When you concentrate on it with a rapt, spiritually listening heart, embracing each note with every sense open and attentive, birdsong will carry you directly into the world of the angels. The angels share a link with birds and birdsong which earthliness cannot sully and the chaotic noise of our modern civilization cannot silence. It will always be magical, and indeed it is magic of the highest order. If you want to enter the fairy worlds, the angelic worlds, whilst still on earth, one certain way to do so is to open your inner ears to birdsong. Follow the example of the abbot of ancient days and lay down your tasks for a moment to listen to it with all your concentration; you will find the same deep enchantment of timelessness and profound renewal as you enter the worlds within. Let Anpiel foster within your soul the love of birdsong and reveal to you its marvel in all its ascending dimensions.

Raphael and Tobias, 1507–8 (oil on panel), by Tiziano Vecelli Titian (c.1488–1576). Galleria dell'Accademia, Venice, Italy/The Bridgeman Art Library

Breakthrough Angel
Ur-i-el

His mode is usually masculine; he is one of the great angels, called 'flame of God' and 'prince of lights'; he is a revealer of mystery to humankind, and his impact is always earth-shattering. There is thunder and lightning in his being; his robes are electric blue, white and bright silver; his perfume is the potent incense rising from votive fires.

Uriel is the breakthrough angel, when to save ourselves we have to move past a great looming fear or an immoveable resistance within ourselves. For instance, loneliness might be a serious issue causing depression, and yet there is a fear of being with others; or a desire to achieve in life, and yet the way is blocked by devastating under-confidence and nervous problems In such cases, the forward route is barred by the indwelling immoveable resistance. Uriel provides the irresistible force that will blast its way through the immoveable object and pulverize its resistance. Of course, he is compassionate, and will blast and pulverize in simple and gentle ways until your road is clear! Nevertheless, the motive force is there. Your first move in releasing yourself from your imprisonment is to call on Uriel; if you will follow him, he will show you an incremental way to freedom.

Angel of the Chaste Hands
Oues-tu-cati

Her mode is usually feminine; known as 'the lady of the chaste hands', she manifests in exquisite beauty and purity. She comes from the Hesperides and brings the invigorating, cleansing sea wind to clear the mind and detoxify the body. Her robes carry the colours of supernaturally beautiful seashells: bright white with pearly depths, sometimes played over by delicate pearline shades of rose-pink, gold, and shining sapphire blue. Her music is the sound of the lullaby of the sea, infused with sirenic voices which soothe the soul into a purifying peace of heart and mind but do not hypnotize or stupefy; her perfume is the fragrance of sea-lavender – mellifluent but with the brace of the ocean's brine in it.

Ouestucati will wash away all defilement and contamination from your hands and from your aura. Call on her to launder all etheric impurities that cling to your hands before and after assuming an important task, such as preparing food or offering care. Just hold out your hands to Ouestucati and slowly turn them around as if washing them as you invoke her and receive her ministrations. If you feel you need an auric cleansing, call her into your centre – your solar plexus – and feel the hub of her influences as she creates a whirlpool of positive, forward-spinning angelic force, energizing, purifying and revitalizing but soothing and harmonious. Simply drawing close to this beautiful angel and bathing in the pearly light of her aura will cleanse you and make you feel better.

Angel of Children
Zo-tiel

Her mode is usually feminine; she is of the order of cherubs, and is known as the 'little one of God'. Zotiel is one of the 'whispering angels' – angels who bring healing and reassurance to those in distress by a constant whispering in the ear of the wisdom and goodness of Divine Spirit, and of the unfailing love and protection of the angels. The colour of her robes is a gentle, radiant rose rippled through by sparkling sunlight; her perfume is that of the fragrance of roses on a warm summer's day, sweet and consoling.

Invoke Zotiel to bring comfort to fearful children, or to adults who are very insecure and timid. She will encourage children's play and help to formulate it so that it banishes fear and builds confidence. She will help you to tune in to a child's wavelength and bring joy and delight to your mutual communion. Call on her whenever you feel disempowered and vulnerable, or you feel a need for the kind of reassurance that a child might receive from a loving adult.

Angel of Clear-Seeing
Zur-iel

His mode is usually masculine; he is associated with the fundament of truth, the foundation-stone of the temple of the soul and the throne or seat of power which informs it. His rays cut a swathe through the clinging mists and glamours of illusion. His robes coruscate with the light of the purest rock crystal, his eyes are the soul of clear quartz translated into angelic dimensions. His music is a constant rhythmic vibration, like the sound of bees deepened and made more reverberant, or Tibetan monks chanting. His perfume is like the zest of lemons, sharp and clarifying.

Call on this prince of angels to help to overcome the mindsets and stumbling blocks that bar your way forward. Zuriel is known as a 'curer of the stupidity in man'. We seek Zuriel's help in illuminating dim spiritual sight and opening spiritually deaf ears. We especially need him when we are disconnected from our soul and the source of its wisdom, the intuition. He comes to our aid when our judgement may be clouded by strong emotion or bias. As communion with him deepens, he signals a warning when deception is being practiced against us.

Angel of Colours
Am-er-e-ton

Her mode is usually feminine; she is one of the 'high, holy angels' who presides over 'Ink and Colours' and who blesses arts and crafts; her evocative breath infuses the Book of Kells and other ancient illuminated manuscripts; her robes are exquisitely translucent, like a miracle, and are played over by mystic lights of many colours as in stained glass windows; her eyes are Madonna blue; her music moves in beautiful, silvery, warm modulations of sound, as if it emanates from soft cymbals and the sweetness of Celtic harps; her perfume is that of moss roses on a balmy summer's evening.

Call on her to bless your artistic endeavours and to help in the choice of spiritually-attuned colours and colour schemes. When you are feeling depressed or disconnected and wish to respond more to the colours around you and the subtle colours of your life's journey, Amereton will offer her angelic aid.

Angel of Companion and Domestic Animals
Hari-el

His mode is usually masculine; his robes are the soft dun colours of the earth, touched with the yellow of sand dunes and the orange of sacred antipodean deserts; he is an angel set over science and the arts, which indicates the inspiration, both spiritual and orthodox, that these disciplines draw from study of the animal kingdom. His music is the springing rhythm of folk and tribal songs; his perfume is the earthy musk ascending from animal-haunted valleys in the rising mists of a warm summer's dawn; he brings healing and protection to pets and farm animals, and shelters them from abuse.

Invoke Hariel on behalf of your companion animal, should any health, training, or psychological problems arise, and for deeper communion with your animal friend. You will delight Hariel if you bless farm animals on your walks or within your contemplations: send a blessing to the pigs and the sheep, the cows and bullocks, the ducks, geese, turkeys and chickens. Especially send a blessing to the victims of slaughterhouses, on their round-up at the farm or market, their journey to their terrible destination (often appalling in the extreme, particularly as animals know they are going to their death) and their ordeal on their arrival, for they are often tortured by workers deranged by the daily tasks they have to perform before they are led to their horrifying deaths. Edward Munch, the artist, painted his depiction of *The Scream*, made famous by the well-known eponymous films, when he saw the astral image of the consciousness of suffering floating above a slaughterhouse. Hariel will speed the arrival of the day when we will no longer consign our animal brethren to these arenas of horror.

Angel of Compassion
Rha-mi-el

Her mode is usually feminine; her wing-beats form spiritual waves of compassion, empathy, mercy, sympathy and gentleness; when a mortal needs to receive these beautiful qualities, or to express them, the angel Rhamiel is at hand to help. Her robes are a delight to view, cascading around her as white and pure mother-of-pearl touched with softest lavender and silver at their outline; a pearly, dreamy radiance that mellows the soul shines from her entire being; her eyes yield a deep, tender, mellifluous light that diffuses the essence of compassion wherever her gaze rests; when you are taken into her embrace, when you hear the sweet poignancy of her music, like melodious distant violins that invoke heart-shed tears, and imbibe her perfume, which is spoken of as 'the fragrance of blessedness exuded by roses as they open to the sun', all resistance to her angelic love melts away, and you find healing in her heart of compassion.

Summon Rhamiel when you need her beautiful gifts, and if you will act as her channel when others need to receive them, you will fill the angels with joy.

Angel of the Cool Brow
La-zai

His mode is usually masculine; he is spoken of as 'a holy angel of God' with mastery over fire and heat-producing ailments; his robes are clear, fluid and pure, like transparent garments of shining water through which his vital inner fires can be seen, playing and coruscating in golden vividness but sealed off by the protective shielding of the cool and gentle water of his garments; his eyes are pools of stillness; his music is the beauty of silence, as though it had fallen as a blessing; his perfume is the musk of ambergris incense.

Call on this serene angel to heal inflammation and heat-producing maladies, or to take the heat out of an uncomfortable or escalating situation.

Angel of Creativity
Ir-el

Irel's mode is divided equally between the feminine and the masculine, and is often androgynous. His robes encompass the whiteness of virgin snow and the molten gold of fire, although violet and indigo hues breathe over them, becoming at last an exquisite hallowed amethyst colour, lit from within by its own secret soft-bright radiance, like a miracle. Irel is of the Ischim, angels composed of snow and fire and resident in the fifth heaven, according to the Psalms. They are angels of the higher graces and their divine task is to sing creation into being via their adoration of the highest of the high. They are linked with the sanctified souls of the saints, and are associated with the light and the power that fortifies this exalted company. Irel's music is the swell of vast choirs pouring forth the 'song celestial'; her perfume is the all-enveloping fragrance of potent lilies.

Contemplate this angel of fire and snow when you wish to stoke inner creative fires. Call on her, call on him, and open your heart and your soul to the stupendous river of fire from snowy heights that will catch you up in its current and infuse you with the power of creativity.

Angel of Crystals and Gemstones
O-ch

His mode is usually masculine; he has a myriad eyes which scintillate brighter than the brilliance of the clearest stars, although when viewed with inner vision he seems to have only two, the others appearing as vivid flashes in his aura. His robes are rainbow-coloured, incandescent with power as though great waterfalls cascaded eternally throughout them; his music is the wild thunder of these ethereal waterfalls which subsides rhythmically into soft silver notes of peace like the poignant fluting of a bird in the last light of evening. His perfume is sharp and pure, reminiscent of the minerals of rain-washed rock.

This angel, whose name is pronounced similarly to the well-known Scottish exclamation, is not unconnected with the mystery of the Gaels. Much esoteric knowledge of 'the underground stream' culminates in Scotland, and the secret of what aborigines call the *mabain* is what Och fosters and shepherds. This is the mysterious force, the God-force within crystals and gemstones that connects with human consciousness so that the God-force

Detail of the Angel, from *The Virgin of the Rocks (The Virgin with the Infant St. John adoring the Infant Christ accompanied by an Angel)*, c.1508 (oil on panel), by Leonardo da Vinci (1452–1519). National Gallery, London, UK/The Bridgeman Art Library

within us is stirred and released. Call on Och when you wish to meditate to find your deeper self, when you wish for insight into the nature and flow of things, when you wish to embrace the spirit of beauty which dwells like a star in the well of the soul, or when you need greater mental precision and clarity.

Angel of Dreams
Y-ah-ri-el

His mode is usually masculine; he is known as a 'healer of hidden wounds' and presides over dreams; he holds dominion over the moon, who is queen of the subconscious realms; he works under the direction of Gabriel; his robes are composed of moonlight and an interweaving, restful darkness – a positive darkness of beauty and hidden wonders; his music is the sweet, otherworldly call of owls; his perfume is the soporific scent of bean–flowers.

Invoke this angel when you need to heal a condition locked in the subconscious, when you need to ease and make gentle unquiet dreams, or when you seek a clearer understanding of a strange or vivid dream.

Angel of Dreams and Aspirations
Ga-bri-el

Her guise is usually feminine; a great archangel of joy and beauty, Gabriel brought the tidings of the Christ child to Mary and pre-pared her womb to receive him. She was intimately associated with John the Beloved Disciple who shared her angelic consciousness, and blessed his mission of bringing hope, truth, justice, revelation, mercy and resurrection to the world, all qualities over which she presides. She was with Jacob as he struggled with his foe on the mountain, for it was Gabriel who tested his strength to ensure that he would be able steadfastly to bear on her torch, although by no means was she herself his 'dark antagonist', as is sometimes claimed. She gave the Koran, '*sura* by *sura*', to Mohammed, who associated her with the Holy Spirit, the feminine Paraclete, although he portrayed her gender as male. According to court transcripts, Gabriel was the angel who inspired Joan of Arc to rescue the declining monarchy of France and lead it in liberating the country. Gabriel's name is inscribed in the oldest records of angels on earth (Chaldean, formerly Sumerian, sources). Her robes are as bright as the full moon, white and shining and touched with silver; her music is the music of rejoicing; her perfume is that of white roses and white lilies.

Gabriel will bless your cherished dreams and aspirations. She knows the very depths of life, and how we all labour to some extent under the power of illusion. She breaks the hold of that illusion and allows your deeper self to step forward and offer its gifts. Don't fear her power of disillusionment, because revelation will follow in its wake. When you bring your dreams and aspirations to Gabriel, she will test them. You may discover that they are dross, which is always disconcerting!

But then Gabriel reveals what your dreams and aspirations truly are, and that moment of revelation is life-changing. Its fruit is Gabriel's gift of radiant happiness.

Angel of Doves
Al-phun

Her mode is usually feminine; she is guardian of the eighth hour, the sigil of the continuous flow of life created by the frequencies of the Sacred Marriage; she presides over doves and the magic and meaning of doves; her robes are of the whiteness of doves; her music is their call; her perfume is of honeyed meads.

This delightful angel, full of a wild sublime sweetness, releases her doves as an uprush of prayer. Call on her to release her beautiful charges in honour of your prayers so that they might be carried to the heart of divinity on the wings of doves. Lovers in particular can pray for the benefit of one another through Alphun's ministrations. You might like to use the figure 8 in your invocation of her, either by using the hour of eight-o'-clock or imagining or inscribing the number in silver, gold or white.

Angel of Edification
Bar-bel-o

Her mode is usually feminine; she is an archon (the highest seat of office) amongst the angelic host, spoken of as 'perfect in glory and next in rank only to the Godhead'. Reference is made to her in the Gnostic *Gospel of Mary Magdalene* and the *Apocryphon of John*, and in other Gnostic texts she is described as the daughter of Pistis Sophia, the angel who emanates the consciousness of Divine Mother. Her robes are shades of heavenly blue, ranging from azure, cerulean and turquoise to robin's egg, peacock and Madonna blue; she wears a jewel of surpassing beauty at her heart; her music is the symphony of the cosmos; her perfume is the perfume of forests and wooded glades, touched with the honey of bluebells rising from the grass beneath the boughs.

Barbelo is an 'educator' angel. Call on her when you seek wisdom and learning, or when your life seems nothing but an obscurity and a source of confusion to you. She will uplift and inspire you to think more in terms of spiritual values and insights. She sheds a golden effulgence onto life's ups and downs, so that the breath and beneficence of Divine Spirit may be sensed through them, leading us home to the light of our eternal selves.

Angel of Emancipation
Joph-i-el

His mode is usually masculine; he is an expansive angel, bright-eyed and humorous; he is known as 'the beauty of God'. His robes are the bright sunshine yellow of joy and exuberance, quietening to the pale pearly buff of the great plains and prairies of the earth where the spirit can roam free in solitude and airy spaces. His music is harmonious and beautiful, but arresting, with much clashing of cymbals and sounding of trumpets. His perfume evokes the image of huge sails on a galleon billowing with the spiced breezes blowing from many lands.

This mighty angel liberates our minds and our outlook from the bonds of programming and conditioning attached to sources which are not in harmony with the wisdom of the soul. He brings us emancipation, enlightenment, and the courage of open-mindedness.

Angel of the Everlasting Arms
Zer-u-el

His mode is usually masculine; his mighty enfolding arms are visible in his sheltering wings; he is an angel 'set over strength', but his 'arms' offer comfort and reassurance and a renewal of strength and trust. They are not the 'arms' of war. His robes are the soft blue of a summer evening sky, drifting into the peaceful violet and amethyst of a gentle radiant twilight in which the first tender stars appear. His music is the sighing and lilt of a soothing fair weather wind; his perfume is the sacred aroma of frankincense.

When you are sad and weary of life, when you need comfort and strength to endure, call on Zeruel, Angel of the Everlasting Arms, the arms that will unfailingly support you and bear you up.

Angel of the Falling Dew
Miri-el

Her mode is usually feminine; she offers the sacred Dew Cup, which contains a drop of the elixir of life, the life that leaps not only in the body but replenishes the mind, heart and soul. It is said of her that she ensouls the dynamic that carries all things new over the spiritual threshold to be birthed into the world. She wears an aura of enrapturing magic and enchantment, the soul-sweetness of wonder. Her robes are mysterious: they are like a fine mist enjewelled with glimmering diamonds of dew that reflect, now the subtle shades of every hue of the rainbow, now the purest moonlight so that she seems bedecked with pearls. She is the spirit of everlasting youth, poised in a radiant living dream of paradise. Her joy is deep and still and is a wellspring she bids you drink from. Her music is like strains of the harp when its notes are most liquid and seem to arise as the spirit of beautiful serene waters. Her perfume is different for each soul that encounters her: the perfume of sacred remembrance, the perfume of all the deepest-loved things, the most cherished times, that return to us borne on a sense of aroma.

The Angel of the Falling Dew comes to you to bring the touch of magic back into your life. She offers succour and renewal when your hopes and dreams have dried up and withered away. She comes to us at our call when we are jaded, when it seems that no greenness or freshness will ever return to our roots or to the ramifications of our inner and outer selves. She personifies the pouring of pure temperate water onto the flower expiring from thirst.

A beautiful story exists in folklore about an angel of benevolence who offered the Dew Cup to all who were weary or sorrowful. The hopeful recipient had only to go to a certain grassy knoll in a wood and call upon the angel for her to appear with her cup of mercy. On one occasion a man who had received the bounty of the cup noticed how beautiful it was, forged from gold and set with jewels. He made a second visit to the knoll and, when the angel appeared, attempted to wrest the cup from her. The angel and the cup vanished, never to appear again, and the wood enshrining the knoll died. Miriel will always come to our aid, but we need to remember to connect deeply with what is essential in our lives when we call on her. Sweep away all trivia, all superficial values, all that doesn't matter, and summon Miriel to replenish you in your depths. Then she can help you to create yourself anew, for she has guardianship over an alchemical dewdrop, distilled from heaven, which can transform human lives.

Angel of Fertility
Yus-a-min

Her mode is usually feminine; one of the three supreme angels of Mandaean scripture, she is an angelic 'spirit of fertility dwelling in the wellsprings of light'; her robes are the colour of 'the pale golden fires of the first hour of morning', vibrant and vividly alight; her music is the fluting of the dawn chorus; her perfume is incense of rose and jasmine.

This shining being may be invoked when we need the blessing of fertility at any level – mentally, emotionally or physically. She works with the Angel of Conception and the Angel of Creativity, although of course she is a supreme force in her own right.

Angel of Fishermen
A-rar-i-el

His mode is usually masculine; he is of the company called 'curers of stupidity in men' and is associated with the mystic concept of 'fishers of souls'; he teachers those who fish for a living or for recreation to understand the deeper aspect of their enterprise and was anciently known as a servant of Oannes, the Fish-Man, who brought enlightenment and civilisation to the earliest human communities. Oannes manifested as a fish-man to show war-loving men that they were sperm in the womb of Divine Mother, and that they were sourced in her and came forth from her. His mission was peace: a peace that Arariel gives to fishermen. His robes are white, shone upon by a golden aura; his music is the music of the sea, both thunderous and softly sighing; his perfume is that of freshly washed linen fragrant with the cleanliness of Paradise.

Call on Arariel pragmatically for a plentiful catch or to reel in a big fish, but also to understand the deepest secrets of our origins. Arariel's code is the ethical treatment of the oceans and the return of freshwater fish to their element whenever it is not vital that they be utilized for food.

Angel of Fortification
Cham-u-el

His mode is usually masculine; his robes shine with the albescence of a swan's breast; he is known as 'white peace'; he stands in his circle of white light, his deep eyes calm as a still and soundless lake, imperturbable, unshakable, invincible. The beautiful angel Chamuel is one of the seven Archangels and chief over the order of angels known as Powers.

He is the angel of Gethsemane, fortifying the Messiah with the assurance of resurrection throughout the watches of the terrible night before the crucifixion. Chamuel is indeed a fortifying angel, bringing strength and resolution with which to face our worst agonies and apprehensions. Yet Chamuel is also an angel of gentleness, reminding us that gentleness is strength. His music moves in slow, deep tones of serene grandeur; his perfume is sandalwood.

Death of a Butterfly, c.1905–10 (oil on canvas), by Evelyn De Morgan (1855–1919). © The De Morgan Centre, London/The Bridgeman Art Library

Call on Chamuel when you need to receive fortifying strength and resolution, and also to inspire tolerance and to soften harsh, critical, antagonistic attitudes. Chamuel not only girds our loins; he helps us to love and to forgive ourselves, and to let go of a judgemental outlook on life, our own failings, and those of other people. Chamuel eases tense, distressed stances deep within the human psyche, especially that of intolerance, so that we can transform inner warring into the deep peace that flows from him.

Angel of Free Will
Tab-ris

His mode is usually masculine; this angel is set over free will, self-determination and independence of choice. His robes are electric blue, the perfection of hue of tropical fish and blue lagoons; his eyes are a deep, striking violet. When you need to gather together the remnants of a scattered, exhausted will, the violet in Tabris's eyes cleanses and integrates your fractured aura like a spiritual laser.

His music is the soft chanting of devotional harmonies; his perfume is sweet-scented thyme, which has a rabbit language★ resonance because those whose will is easily drained often have an afflicted relationship with time.

Tabris shows you how to direct the energy flow within you so that its frequencies do not jam one another.

Invoke Tabris when you need help to lift yourself out of a stalemate or stuck situation and seek to become aware of creative alternatives. Call on him when you feel disempowered and cannot muster your free will, as though adversarial forces, or perhaps someone else's will, were separating you from it. Tabris will quietly restore the reins of direction and pace to your hands. Remem-

---

★ The 'rabbit language' is a native and instinctive Mother Tongue of the earth, in which you 'mark what you see' in the formation of words.

ber Colopatiron, the angel who comes to unlock the prison gate. Tabris and Colpatiron work together. They also grant mortals the necessary patience and endurance to wait quietly and alertly for that moment when their release comes.

Angel of Friendship
Mihr (Mi-er)

His mode is usually masculine; he is spoken of as an 'angel of affection' and is invoked in cases of dissension between mortals; he is also called an 'angel of mercy'; his robes are bright yellow–golden; his eyes catch their colour and gently radiate compassion and understanding like a balm, which he directs into the hearts of those he serves; he is often seen in the midst of a circle of dancing children or cherubs; his music is soothing, with cascading piano-like notes of great purity and a soft murmuring drumbeat.

This luminary has dominion over cooperation and the form-ation of friendship and loving bonds between people. He nurtures the establishment of harmonious relationships. Where difficulties in these areas arise, invoke his help. Call on his powers and bless-ings in establishing your relationships. Mihr, Omniel, and Itkal work together, and can be summoned together with prayer and invocation. Pray to Mihr to heal rifts between friends, and also to heal an inability to make friends.

Angel of Fruitfulness
Ana-hita

Her guise is usually feminine; she is known as 'the immaculate one, genius of fertilizing water and the fruitfulness of the earth', and 'angel of brightest magnitude and unconscionable beauty'.

She has guardianship of the creative forces on earth, and is a caretaker of the earth and her fecundity. She is therefore mistress of exalted sexuality. Her robes are purest, brightest gold with a touch of emerald at her heart; beautiful and radiant, she seems to move in vivid white clouds of virgin ether; her music is the warbling of songbirds; her perfume is that of apple blossom.

Call on her to invoke blessing for your sexual self, and to understand its deep-fathomed nature. Anahita nurtures fruitfulness and flowering at every level. Especially she blesses those who love the natural world and the planet and express that love. You can also pray to her to heal the earth, or any part of it which has become barren or distressed.

Angel of the Fruits of the Earth
Sof-i-el

Her mode is usually feminine; she has particular guardianship over the fruits and vegetables of the earth, helping them to flourish and keep healthy. Her garments are as many-coloured as summer: sunlit colours of bounty and happiness; her eyes smile with an infectious lightness of heart, and yet there is a profound silence and stillness within them; her hair is like a golden joyful outpouring from the heart of the sun; her music is the music of piping, fiddles and drums; her perfume is the scent of blossom in full bloom.

Sofiel is also a wonderful grounding angel, and will reconnect sick and depleted mortals to vital earth energies. When you sense a blockage or a lack of the upflowing forces from the earth in your spirits or your aura, call on Sofiel. She will remind you that there is always a paradise to be found in every human heart, no matter how constricted its scope for expression in the outer life.

Angel of Grace
An-an-chel

Her mode is usually feminine; her robes are spring green with soft, mystic glitters of emerald in their depths; her movement and the folds of her wings are like the quavering dance of the Northern Lights, for she embraces her invocants from above; her eyes are a tender outpouring of grace, like the light from the first stars in the blue twilight of a spring evening; her music is the sound of ethereal flutes, like a fairy piper; her perfume is the scent of abundant lilac blossoms borne on the breast of a gentle wind.

Call on the magic and beauty of Ananchel when you are in need of grace, perhaps because you have an important task to undertake or a difficult duty to fulfill. Whatever your situation or predicament, remember Ananchel; she will fill your empty cup and grant you, by grace, whatever you feel you lack. Ananchel is also the angel of gracefulness, of poise. Her dance is the sky dance of the Aurora Borealis. Dancers and performers will benefit from invoking her help. When you seek grace of speech, of movement, of living, Ananchel will come to your aid.

Angel of Gardens
Cah-eth-el

His mode is usually masculine; he is one of the eight seraphim and bears the holy name throughout his being; he fosters agriculture and blesses gardens, weaving the love of humans and the love of nature spirits for the garden within his own angelic love to create wonder, beauty and peace in its dimensions, however small; his robes are viridian green; his music is the chant and hum of 'goodly insects' such as bees and crickets: when transposed to a higher level, these insects sing in magnificent symphonies, which resonate from him; his perfume is the scent of new-mown hay.

Pray to this guardian angel of gardens when you wish to invoke blessings on a garden or the creation of a garden, or healing for a struggling or infested garden. Remember, too, the gardens of the mind that bring the peace of paradise to your soul when you need spiritual refreshment. The writer Katherine Mansfield wrote that she could lie back and watch gardens of sublime beauty float through her mind. These gardens of the mind are for our healing and revivification. To our limited perception of reality they are insubstantial, but that is an illusion. They are real.

Angel of Good Thought
Vo-hu Ma-nah

Her mode is usually feminine; this almighty angel enfolds us in great wings of softest blue, like a perfect summer sky. Vohu Manah actually gathers us up into the blue, as though we are taken right into the eternal deeps of the smiling blue sky; she is the personification of 'good thought' or God-thought'. Queen of the archangels, traditionally she receives souls into heaven, but in fact she can lift us into the higher realms without the inconvenient intervention of death! If we accept her gifts, she becomes the Angel of Ascension. Her music is the cascading song of the skylark; her perfume is the honey of the date.

This wonderful angel blesses and uplifts our thoughts and our thought-sphere (the vessel which generates, contains, attracts, reflects and distributes our thoughts). If we suffer from a negative, anxious or pessimistic outlook, or tend to generate otherwise inharmonious thought energy, especially about others, we need to be brought into the healing presence of Vohu Manah. Opening to the inflow of angelic consciousness with all the blessing, inspiration and healing it brings, cannot be achieved without the attuning power of the positive vibrations of 'good thought' that Vohu Mana so lovingly enshrines, nurtures and bestows. This beneficent one ignites and fosters the beautiful flame of happy, positive and loving thoughts, feelings and impulses in our mind, heart and soul.

Angel of Gratitude
Shem-a-el

His mode is usually masculine; he is spoken of as standing at the windows of heaven, transfixed with delight and compassion as he listens to the prayers of love for Divine Spirit ascending from humanity below; his robes shine with the translucence of gems from the angelic worlds; his music is the sound of ethereally sweet violins with the keening of a horn echoing through them; his perfume is frankincense.

Shemael fosters the upwelling of gratitude in the human heart. When these springs have run dry or become choked, depression and a feeling of disgust with life is the inevitable result. Energy does not replenish itself, and a person may put on weight in an attempt to draw mental and physical energy from food and the act of eating. When life seems grey, desolate and grief-stricken, it is difficult to feel gratitude for the experience of it. Therefore, we treat depressive, world-weary feelings with Shemael's gentle, compassionate gifts, so that the deep wellsprings of the spirit may be renewed. Call on Shemael whenever you feel stony-hearted and unrelenting, and wish to be released from the stubborn prison that has formulated itself around you. He will help you to express thankfulness as well as to feel it.

Angel of Hailstorms
Bar-di-el

His mode is usually masculine; he has a cyclonic energy and whirring wings; his colour is that of swan feathers touched with a soft wild-dove grey; his perfume is sharp, like that of storm winds across the sea.

Call on Bardiel to ease the hail shower, to gentle the storm. Send gentleness to him and he will infuse it into his manifestations. This human soothing fills him with joy. He is a shaker- and a stirrer-up, so imbibe his energies if you are feeling lifeless, lethargic and unenthused! You don't need to wait for a hailstorm to bathe in his influences, but use them with caution and wisdom.

Angel of Harmony
It-qual

Her mode is usually feminine; her robes are a soft clear amber, with a depth of peace in them; she radiates unobtrusive good cheer and well-being, and has golden smiling eyes over which the spirit of kindly laughter plays; she works with Camaysar, the Angel of the Marriage of Contraries, to perfect her tasks; her perfume is that of honey with a palpable silken quality, as though it caresses your skin and reaches the part of you in dissonance so that aggrieved feelings melt away.

Invoke Itqual when family disputes and squabbles occur or where estrangement has asserted itself. Work with her in conjunction with Camaysar. Itqual is one of the 'whisperers', the 'little ones of God' (although mighty in her service) who murmurs positive, soothing, beautiful truths into the ears of those she serves so that their sickness of disharmony and contentiousness is healed.

Tobias and the Angel, 15th century (oil on panel),
by Altobello Meloni (fl.1497–1517). Ashmolean Museum,
University of Oxford, UK / The Bridgeman Art Library

Angel of Healing
Raph-a-el

His mode is sometimes masculine, sometimes feminine; his form is mighty, as tall as a cathedral.

His eyes shine with loving compassion, emitting a great light, and yet they are as mellow and gentle and deep as the glow of ancient and mysterious gold. His melodious mouth utters rhythmic healing chants, beautiful in their vibration, becoming from time to time a great burst of exquisite song which pierces the listening soul with an irresistible tide of love as renewal, as reawakening, as revivification. There is the fragrance of cleansing joy in the robes of Raphael, and golden healing in his wings. The perfume he emits is that of sweet-smelling herbs.

Bathe in the healing light of Raphael, just for joy, because there is true magic in it. Hear his soft chanting and his burst of song through which the cadence of the word 'Consolamentum' ('the Comforter') beats like a spirit drum, and feel all your energies in all your bodies – mind, emotion, soul and physical – rise as if newborn from an ocean of sparkling drops of the utmost purity, rise in new white garments to the blazing disc of the morning sun. Raphael's golden wings of light enfold you in their great arcs of sweeping spiritual force, and you know yourself as perfect in light, perfect within the sunlight of his healing embrace. Rest in that perfect light, fresh and revitalized, created anew.

Angel of the Helping Hand
I-ad-i-el

Her mode is usually feminine; we have only scant knowledge of Iadiel; she is known as the 'little mysterious one' and the 'Hand of God'. It is as if she hides in the ethers, only showing herself for a split second whilst performing her duties. There is something very intriguing and delightful about her, as if she were a shy wild creature among the angels!

She appears when you are without the help you need to do or to complete something important, urgent or significant, or just practically necessary. You may well call on other angels, angels of protection, angels of strength, angels of inspiration and grace; but do not forget Iadiel, the 'little mysterious one', the 'Hand of God'. The help you need will appear, sometimes quite startlingly, sometimes disguised, so it is necessary to keep your mind and eyes wide open and sharp whenever you request it; but come it will.

Angel of Heroes
Nars-in-ha

His mode is usually masculine; he manifests as a man-lion, a great angel with the head of a lion, yet of a man; he was known to the ancients as 'lord of heroism' and was associated with the constellation of Leo; his robes are fiery golden and ripple like the flanks of a lion; blazing auriferous rays surround his head; his amber eyes are kindly, yet press us on to go for the mark; he exudes great heat, which is not uncomfortable but enwraps the human heart in the reassurance of warmth, confidence and courage; his music is the great rumble of organs (Bach was inspired by Nar-sin-ha and once walked a hundred miles to view a particular church organ – certainly a heroic feat); his perfume is the musk of great plains and airy open spaces surrendering their honeyed aromas as the morning sun strikes them so that their dews become ether and release their fragrance.

Call on Narsinha whenever you need courage and determination to follow through, to complete a task or begin some challenging endeavour. At times a surpassingly beautiful feminine lion comes forth from him, as if stepping out of his heart. Narsina then becomes this feminine wonder.

The exalted frequency and consciousness she exudes is heart-stopping in its loveliness, awe-inspiring and humbling. Around her head is an aureole of pulsating gold, which suggests to me that the mane of the male lion is present in females but is ethereal rather than physical. Narsinha has a great roar which, on invoking him, resounds throughout the soul when we are grasping after courage but are feeling fractious and fainting. The roar pulsates through us like a vigorous inner massage and vibrates at our very roots, giving us strength to see off the crowding elementals of doubt, fear, worry and complaint.

Angel of the Hills
Lu-mar

Lumar usually manifests in androgynous mode; she is named among the 'splendid, terrible and mighty angel chiefs' who passed before God to extol and rejoice in the bringing forth of Creation; he lifts our vision to the hilltops and to heaven; her robes are the blue of boundless meditation: the blue of distant hills; his music is the movement of mighty symphonies; her perfume is the scent of Cypress touched with the incense of rosewood.

Call on this angel when you need a higher perspective. Whenever your vision seems fettered, earthbound and narrow, when you feel pettiness and confusion pressing in on you, look to the Angel of the Hills. If your life seems squalid or pointless, when you feel the dragging pull of minutiae, when you feel enslaved by circumstances or relationships, look to the Angel of the Hills. The help you need – the discernible door, the fresh air, the new perspective – will come.

Angel of Hoarfrost
Kara-Dia

Her mode is usually feminine; her robes are like cobwebs filtering moonlight; her eyes are bright as diamonds, with a spirit of wildness in them and a strange fixity; she brings forth angelic loveliness out of deathly cold, capturing the astral forms of flowers and the ethereal configurations of the spirit of life in a transient fixation of ice and snow so that we can perceive them with physical eyesight; her music is a distant, barely discernible tinkling, poignant and lonely and infused with the spirit of the wilderness.

Kara Dia teaches us how to look with the eyes of the spirit through our bodily eyes. She delineates the intricacy of the beauty of natural forms, tracing their material outline and incarcerating the delicacy of their elusive informing spirit for a little while in frost so that we may see and experience them. Call on her when your thoughts are straining after some inchoate, semi-realised thought or perception: when you are trying to recall a dream, or capture an inspiration, or snatch some passing half-heard song out of the air before it eludes you, either to remember it or compose it. Kara Dia helps composers, artists, writer, poets, thinkers. She serves all creative tasks. Her breath is breath of ice, but it is the breath of love. Whenever you cannot quite grasp your inspiration, when it dances enthrallingly in the heart but will not come to mind, invoke Kara Dia to encapsulate it with her breath. Then take it into your heart with the vehicle of your mind and breathe warmth into it. It is yours.

Angel of Hope
Phan-u-el

His mode is usually masculine; he is a fiery angel, giving off light like a bright golden star, and yet a flame burns still and resolute in his depths, inextinguishable and lovely; he is a tall and encompassing angel; his wings seem to lift his invocants into new vistas and brighter climes so that in turn their vision can grow new wings. His music is bright and uplifting, strains from heaven with the sound of silvery bells in its wandering airs; his perfume is bergamot.

Don't be afraid to call on the Angel of Hope constantly whenever you feel that slump inside which signals that your inner buoyancy is fading. When we are without hope we lead dead, embittered lives. Phanuel is eager to give you a generous transfusion of hope whenever you are in need of it.

Angel of Hymns, Invocations and Prayer
Vri-has-pati

Her mode is usually feminine; she is beloved of mystics and visionaries, who call her 'first-born in the highest Heaven of supreme light'. Her robes are the colour of summer skies transmuting into the skies of Paradise in shades of sweet, heavenly cerulean blue; all the hues of beautiful skies drift through her ethereal garments; the crimson and orange of sunset are sometimes present, the soft rose and clear celandine gold of dawn, the luminous green and hushed lavender of dusk in the last poignant western light of the far heavens at the day's farewell: all these belong to Vrihaspati.

Her music is a crescendo of beautiful song like a peal of celestial bells; her perfume is a cascade of fragrance from Paradise.

Guardian of hymns, invocations and prayers, this venerable one fosters, shepherds and inspires our aspirations towards the spiritual realms.

We can call on Vrihaspati to bless our prayers and invocations and help us to formulate new ones which are beautiful and effective and which please the angels. This angel also gives profound and lovely impetus to the wordless hymns to beauty and to nature and to the experience of love that can fill us and rise from us like 'plumes of light', according to angel-seers. Vrihaspati frees our soaring soul so that we may 'laugh all of our laughter, and weep all of our tears' and know no failure of consummation with the higher vistas and the deeper worlds beyond the common light of day.

Angel of Ice
Iz-la

His guise is usually masculine; his robes are the diffusion of many colours: pale, delicate glitterings like the hues seen through ice; his music is mighty, like ice-floes breaking up; his perfume can be sensed on the winter wind when ice and snow cover the landscape – sharp, bracing and vigorously pure.

Call on Izla to soothe and gentle the winter blast. Send easing and warmth to him, and he will soften the grip of the wild and extreme weather. He will exult in working with you to bring this about. His deeper purpose is to bring to human attention the principles of ice and fire from which the cosmos creates itself. He tells us that when spirit or the hand of God united the two, a fire-mist was born which formed the worlds.

He works with the Angel of Hoarfrost to bring us gifts from the past, touching unheated windows with a rime and frost that show us the ethereal forms of the very early plant life on our earth – the spirits of nature which propagated the first trees and gave birth to vegetation. We will see in the mystic patterns of the ice the primal fern-fronds that formed the primeval forests. The principles of ice and fire are governed by the angels, but they need human consciousness to find the point of balance between them so that wonders and marvels may come into being and the joy of harmony may be attained. He will help you to integrate extremes and discover that point of ineffably creative balance between polarities. Its location is in the human heart.

Angel of the Imagination
Sam-an-dir-i-el

Samandiriel's mode is androgynous; he is the bright angel of the imagination, clear as mirrored jewels. There is a perfume of spice when Samandiriel is near, and a music as of wind in the reeds.

Call on Samandiriel to awaken and vivify your imagination. It is one of the most powerful tools you possess, and will open to you every level of the 'house of many mansions'.

Angel of Integrity
Haa-mi-ah

Her mode is usually feminine; she is an angel of truth and integrity; her robes fan out like a flare of purifying light; her music is arresting, like sweet trumpets; her perfume is the fragrance of subtle spicy ginger.

Call on Haamiah whenever you feel the need to protect or restore your integrity. To receive her kiss is to receive a brand of light that pierces every dimension of the soul. It causes no distress, but rather a wonderful release of confusion, a clearing away of unwise accumulation. When we withhold honesty from ourselves or others, it harms the soul. A mist covers our feelings and our relationships with others – a confusing, distressing mist that makes everything, life's normal dynamics, seem stressful and traumatic. If

Annunciatory Angel, 1450–55 (gold leaf and tempera on wood panel), by Fra Angelico (Guido di Pietro) (c.1387–1455). Detroit Institute of Arts, USA/ Bequest of Eleanor Clay Ford/The Bridgeman Art Library

you have lost sight of your own truth and you feel the resultant pull away from your centre, your integrity, call this angel into your field of spiritual vision with a sincere prayer for help. She will restore you to yourself.

Angel Healer of Jealousy and Resentment
Bal-thi-el

His mode is usually masculine; he is known as a great cosmic angel, one of the seven planetary spirits; according to Solomon and Enoch, he is 'the only angel who is able to overcome or thwart the machinations of the evil genius of jealousy'; his robes are a rich sunlight green, the hue of the burgeoning quality that trees take on when they are in full leaf, played over by an ethereal angelic gold; his eyes are radiant windows of pure emerald; his music is tripping and joyous, with beautiful healing strains in its dimensions which are solemn and majestic; his perfume is oil of cypress.

This mighty angel helps us to overcome jealousy, and feelings of inadequacy, bitterness and resentment. Call on him whenever you feel the encroachment of these miserable feelings.

Angel of Just Causes
Nem-am-i-ah

His mode is usually masculine; he has almost a military bearing, and his apparel, which is white, suggests the impression of a uniform with silver buttons, although there is free flow and grace to his garments and he has a warm golden aura. He has been called the 'good soldier's angel', presiding over admirals, generals and all warriors of true moral bearing. His music is the music of marches; his perfume is a blend of frankincense and cardamon, warm and reassuring.

You can invoke Nemamiah to heal an injustice, especially one dealt out to the frail and the vulnerable, whether human or animal, and to bless any worthy cause your path might lead you to undertake. However, it is worth remembering that Nememiah works on behalf of selfless causes. If you feel that you are a victim of injustice, call on Ach-Sah, the Angel of Benevolent Outcomes, rather than Nememiah.

Angel of Kindness
Ha-el

Her mode is usually feminine; she is an angel of art and beauty who inspires mercy and kindness to flourish in human hearts; her robes are translucent shades of rose and amethyst; her touch is soft as rose petals, yet strengthening and warm, driving the darkness away to vanishing point; there is a sublime exudation of light from her heart that gives nourishment, like the milk of human kindness, in which she bathes the vulnerable who reach out to her; her music is the song of soothing choirs sounding forth hymns of love; her perfume is the fragrance of rose and lavender, with hints of a scent from paradise stealing through it.

Call on Hael when you feel in need of mercy and kindness, either as virtues within yourself or as blessings in your life. Emmanuel Swedenborg, a Swedish scientist who wrote many books about angels, reported a remarkable truth which was imparted to him by his angel friends: that we can see angels according to the extent that we develop and express kindness.

Angel of Languages
Kirt-a-bus

Her mode is usually feminine; her robes are pastel shades of peach deepening into orange; she is aligned to the 'Watchers', the angels, spirits and souls who descended to earth to teach humankind sacred secrets relating to government, education, medicine, agriculture, law, the meaning of the stars and the formulation of languages; her music is the rustling melody of leaves in a vast forest; her perfume is that of orange groves.

Summon her when you are learning a language, when you need greater facilitation in understanding or picking one up abroad, or when you need a deeper and more comprehensive understanding of your native tongue. Thank her with 'Namaste', the universal salutation.

Angel of Leadership
Ya-ho-el

His guise is usually masculine; his brow is powerfully radiant, and he sustains his measureless force by the potency of the ineffable name (his knowledge of God) that dwells within him; one of the great angels, he guides the leaders of humanity; his robes are incandescent with the radiant might of suns; his music is titanic, like that of Beethoven; his perfume is the fragrance of Cedar wood.

Call on Yahoel when you need to express leadership qualities in your own life, or to bestow blessings on a leader in your own community or workplace. Pray to this mighty one if you are working to heal a political or environmental situation which hangs on the making of wise decisions by those in positions of leadership.

Angel of Leading Light
Brig-id

Her mode is feminine; supreme among the beings of the brilliant light of the Ineffable, both angel and goddess, Brigid is the Bride, the Immortal Daughter of the Divine. This golden one, Mistress of the Beings of Inconceivable Fire, brings a burgeoning abundance of healing to humankind of body, mind and spirit. She appears as a measurelessly radiant woman of lustral flame, giving forth her joy, compassion and love, and the strength and inspiration of her spirit, to all humanity. Brigid overlights the divine feminine in us all. She was known to her people – once the inhabitants of the whole of Britain and Ireland as well as many on the continent – as the Woman of Compassion, the Woman of Healing, the Woman of Inspiration, the Woman of Highest Purity, the Woman of Miracles. 'The encompassment of Brigid, Bride of the golden hair, guarding the hearth, guarding the door, guarding the household all' is an old prayer-affirmation from the Scottish Western Isles invoking her protection. Her music can hardly be described, but is something like the voice of the deepest organ played over by the sweetest violins, with ethereal chimes as of bells from heaven sounding subtly in their backdrop. Her perfume is the spiritual essence of the rose, penetrating beyond the rose of Paradise to the mystical rose in God's heart. 'Far off, most secret, and inviolate Rose/ Enfold me in my hour of hours' sang the poet W.B. Yeats in his work, *The Secret Rose*. The secret rose, the rose of God's heart, is Brigid.

Brigid will indeed be your guiding light if you choose to call on her. She will give you protection, offer you guidance, and bring you an inner peace and nurturing that has to be experienced to be understood. She is the Woman of Compassion. Bring her your woes, and be healed.

Angel Healer of Loneliness
Om-n-iel

His mode is usually masculine; he is an angel who fosters our connectedness with one another; he lifts us into Divine Oneness and heals our tendency towards isolation of self; his robes are a warm, pure scarlet, the colour of universal love; his music is the sound of exultant choirs; his perfume is the fragrance of pine resin.

Those suffering from loneliness, from autism, from imbalances in the ego, will benefit from the healing influences of this shining one. It is a maxim of ancient knowledge that loneliness breaks spiritual law, which is probably not the most helpful nugget of wisdom to offer lonely people! The angels are filled with delight when we help someone out of their sad prison of loneliness. Although we can only give general help from a spiritual standpoint unless we have sought permission to be more specific, it is always good to send the blessing of Omniel to those who seem lonely and isolated. Call on Omniel, the Angel of Connectedness, whenever the shades of loneliness threaten to close in on your own life. He will awaken and revitalize the cords that link you to others.

Angel of May (Well-being, Joy and Creative Energy)
Am-briel

Ambriel's mode is usually feminine; she is associated with the Sacred Feminine and with the holy spirit and the holy breath; her robes are alight with numerous dancing colours, for she has dominion over fairy life (the inspiration for 'fairy lights' was taken direct from ancient sightings of the fairy clans, which often manifested as a moving mass of tiny lights, either many coloured or pure white); her music is the wonder of birdsong; her perfume is the perfume of the may, enchanted, occult and heady with the magic of secrets.

Attune gently and harmoniously with Ambriel, establishing communion through the heart. The best time is May-time, when even the dew is said to be infused with enhanced magical properties. Chant her name with spiritual intent and let the joy and sweetness and well-being of the Sacred Feminine enter your soul. Breathe in the holy breath, the enchanted spirit, of May-time. Ambriel will offer her ethereal baptism of the Earth's delight. And then, throughout the year, whenever you need to receive those waters again into your deeper self, whenever you need something to dance into being and blossom within, return to Ambriel's embrace and drink deep.

Angel of Meditation
I-a-hel

Her mode is usually feminine; on observing her, the impression is of a white flame shining in a halo of clear light; beyond this image, she appears as if clad in a cloak of purest swan feathers; she presides over philosophers, mystics, poets and bards: all who need to withdraw from worldly concerns to discover the treasury of the worlds within. Iahel, the lovely angel of meditation and illumination, bestows the grace of her radiance in a shedding of starry light that flashes with points of coruscating illumination. These intense jewel-points of light catch up our human intuition in their fiery dance, energizing and releasing its potential. The picture is of scattered jewels, strewn with love for our soul release. 'Iahel, illustrious lamp of the sacred inner halls, shine in me', sings one invocant. Her music is an angelic call from the inner worlds, filled with the aural lustre of beauty and joy. Her perfume is frankincense and balm.

Pray to this Mistress of the Halls of Boundless Light for depth, clarity and guidance along the path of truth in your meditations. Call on her if you experience any difficulty in meditating, or, if it is not a regular practice, you wish to make it so. Just gaze into her white flame in its aura of clear light, think of a simple word or theme that lies gently in the mind, and keep a quiet inner focus on your chosen point of exploration. When your mind wanders or becomes restless, bring it back to its focus with firm but kindly insistence, ignoring its squirms and attempts to escape! Gradually, and especially with Iahel's assistance, these little bursts of mental rebellion will cease, and your true journeying will begin. You will find that Cosmiel, Angel of Voyaging, will be ready and waiting for you on the other side of the door you have passed through.

Angel of Memory
Zach-ri-el

His mode is usually masculine; his robes are brilliant with ethereal mirrors that have no hardness but are like pools of bright water where pure mists of dimension come and go; his music is the sound of soft melodious echoes as of drops falling into a deep well; his perfume is that of sun-warmed rosemary.

Zachriel will sharpen a sluggish memory and give aid in learning words, figures or sequences by heart, but his loveliest service is to return to us our most poignant and evocative memories, some of which may seem summoned from another life or sphere. There is an element of time travel involved in his powers, and when enfolded in his influence you may find yourself able to remember eras outside the span of your experience as well as episodes from your current life. Zachriel is deeply attuned to the Recording Angel and can help you to unlock buried memories for the sake of their healing and resolution. Remembrance is the magical act of summoning the past into the present. 'Have you remembrances,

An Angel, 1525 (fresco), by Bernardino Luini (c.1480–1532). Sanctuary of the Blessed Virgin of Miracles, Saronno, Italy/The Bridgeman Art Library

the glimmering arches that span the summits of the mind?' asks Gibran in *The Prophet*. There is in 're-member-ing' the notion of bringing a divided body back to wholeness so that all its members function within its harmonious integrity. Zachriel lifts bright gifts of memory from your night-time dreams so that your life can become inspired and visionary. An aborigine poet, Odgeroo Noonuccal, said' 'The past is all about us and within.' Zachriel illumines, restores and empowers it so that it a vehicle of motive force and not a treacherous marsh in which we become trapped and lost.

Angels of Mercy
Rah-mi-el, Rach-mi-el, Ga-bri-el, Mi-cha-el, Zad-ki-el, Ze-han-pury-u

The Angels of Mercy are androgynous (as are all angels, although they appear in masculine or feminine guise according to the particular task they undertake).

To invoke them in this special grouping you need only call their collective name, although chanting the individual names is also helpful. Think of Rahmiel in shades of violet and gentle amethyst, Rachmiel in robes of glowing sunrise rose, Gabriel in soft silver-white, Michael in robes of glorious gold, Zadkiel clad in deep shades of violet and Zehanpuryu enrobed in deep, calming blue. The perfume of the Angels of Mercy is the perfume of the rose.

Invoke the Angels of Mercy if you are in a physical, nervous, psychological or spiritual situation you cannot bear. For every grade of suffering, the Angels of Mercy will come at your call. Send them to family and friends in need, or to animals and beings of nature such as trees and plants if you sense that they are in distress. Sites, buildings, organizations, can receive the help of the Angels of Mercy, or situations such as a famine or war zone. The angels deeply appreciate your inventiveness and out-of-the-box thinking in calling on their help, and they rejoice in being thus summoned.

Angel of Miracles
Mum-i-ah

His mode is usually masculine; it is said of him that he 'controls the science of physics and medicine' and that he is also in charge of health and longevity; because of his profound alchemical knowledge he can 'suspend' the known laws of time and matter to procure miracles. His robes are of soft misty grey with sparkles as of pure quartz crystal moving through them; his heart and eyes are golden; his music is that of mathematical formulae, like the pure springs issuing from the music of Bach, clear and awe-inspiring; his perfume is reminiscent of eucalyptus oil.

Call on Mumiah to help you to understand the workings of life. In certain circumstances you may stand in need of a miracle. Divine Spirit alone grants miracles, but Mumiah serves Divine Spirit so that miracles appear. Mumiah teaches that we live in a scientific universe where the integrity of principles and laws are expressed to utter perfection, but that science is an outflow of the marvel of God, and that so far we have not even begun to grasp its meaning or what it truly is.

Angel of Moonlight
O-fan-i-el

His mode is usually masculine, he works under the direction of Gabriel, who is Angel of the Moon; he serves the fairy kingdom as well as the world of mortals, for fairies bathe in moonlight for revivification; his robes are of ripples of moonlight as though it danced on waters; his music is the sound of fairy pipers and distant, poignant sweet-pealing bells; his song is a wild, high, lovely strain of the solitudes, weaving sorrow and joy into a white flame of beauty; his perfume is a stealing of enchantment over the senses, like the fragrance of may trees on a balmy spring night.

If you leave a glass of spring water on an interior window ledge all night at the time of the full moon, Ofaniel will infuse it with his magical influences. Drink it the next day, and you will literally imbibe his energies!

Bathe your soul in the moonlight, enter into its magic by attuning to Ofaniel, and he will reveal a world of wonder in its sublime beams.

Angel of Music
Is-ra-fel

His mode is usually masculine; his robes make him appear to be the Angel of the Rainbow, for they flow and dance around him in its seven lovely hues, and, tremulous and just on the edge of vision, there are other nameless colours present in his garments, colours that appear and fugitively disappear within a bathing of rapturous light that shines through and beyond his marvellous apparel, which is an outflow from his soul.

Israfel, the beautiful Angel of Music, is the personification of healing. Rhythmically, lyrically, harmoniously, he regenerates, resurrects and renews with his exquisite art which enchants and transfigures the soul and releases the spiritual fires within. In ancient Arabian lore he is 'the burning one', the angel of resurrection and song who will sound the trumpet on the last day of the earth, after which he will be consumed in the fires of sacrifice so that the planet may ascend to a higher dimension. This special element of self-giving led Poe, whose biography by Hervey Allen is entitled *Israfel*, to say lyrically of him … 'the angel Israfel, whose heart strings are a lute, and who has the sweetest voice of all God's creatures.'

Call on Israfel when you sense the presence of broken harmony and broken rhythm, either in yourself, those to whom you are connected, or the environment. Invoke him, too, to hear the secret, hidden music in nature, in the land and the sky, the sea and the hills, the rocks and stones and all growing things. When you listen to beautiful music, especially music composed by the masters but in all music that touches the soul, Israfel will bring the angels of music close to you to weave their creative and transformative magic in dreaming configurations around and throughout the dimensions of your being.

Learn to recognise and welcome Israfel's angels of music; they will always approach and draw close whenever you open your deeper self to their world of sound and harmony.

Angel of Nourishment
Is-da

Her guise is usually feminine; the shining darkness of the night sky is this angel's light, and her dark eyes are deep as oceans beating on virgin shores that harbour undiscovered mysteries. She is spoken of as belonging to the Citadel of the Higher Graces, and her lovely office is to provide nourishment to human beings. She commands one of the Four Hallows of the Holy Grail – that of nourishment – and symbolises ever-replenished bounty. Her music is the sound of the wind in the reeds; her perfume is the fragrance of the earth in its free-handed giving.

Call on Isda when you need to receive nourishment for the body, the mind, the soul or the spirit. She will inspire you in every area of nourishment, from the practical level of life to the most profound and sublime. Send the nourishment she gives by your own act of intention to the sick, the needy, the deprived. She will give to you, and through you.

Angel of Oracles
Phal-dor

His mode is usually masculine; his robes are as if made of flashing mirrors; his eyes seem to hold the stars; his perfume is the scent of lilies of the valley.

The Angel of Oracles gives protection when you use divination. This can be an obsessive practice and can be used unwisely. Phaldor advises the use of oracles only when we are confused as to where to turn and need some words of comfort or direction. He shields our minds from undesirable influences to which we can sometimes become open when using divination. It can be counter-therapeutic to know the future before it happens. The wisest words I have heard on this subject, spoken by a single mother battling her own and her child's serious health problems, are: 'No-one knows what the future may bring; take it a day at a time, and make sure you have a happy day.'

Angel of Order
Sa-dri-el

His guise is usually male; he has huge, encompassing wings, and eyes whose gaze takes away excitability and the urge to rebel or posture egotistically; he calms, sobers, and inspires humility; his robes are orange and golden; his eyes are ancient, like old gold; his perfume is that of myrrh.

Call on Sadriel when you feel you are lacking order in your life, or when it is a quality that you need to maintain, such as in teaching, military, and policing professions, positions of leadership or simply the head or joint head of a family. Sadriel helps to impose order so that the ordered do not feel oppressed! Instead, they tend to respect you for performing a service you need to give. Sadriel may also be invoked for tasks of setting all in order at home or in the office.

Angel of Patience
A-chai-ah

Her mode is usually feminine; she suggests golden horizons and the jewel in the lotus, for these treasures cannot be realised without resonating with her; she is also a 'discoverer of the secrets of nature'. Teresa of Avila referred to her when she wrote 'Patience attains all that it waits for'. Her robes are the colour of a calm blue ocean; her song is an ever-resonant 'om'; her perfume is lavender, sage and thyme.

Whenever you feel the strain of impatience, call on the loveliness and serene centredness of Achaiah, beautiful angel of patience. You may find that you need to invoke this tranquil angel as a daily tonic!

Angel of Peace
Val-oh-el

Her mode is usually feminine; she is a serene brooding presence of softest blue; sometimes she is of pure, ineffable white, like a supernatural dove or a swan which has become an angel; she is the sublime Angel of Peace, with healing in her wings and the balm of tranquillity in her outstretched hands. She is spoken of as the Sister of Silence. Her music is soft and rich, like the mellifluent song of birds when it deepens and sweetens towards the fall of twilight; her perfume is otto of roses.

We can call on this great one to bless us with a serene mind, a tranquil heart and peaceful dreams. We can also ask Valohel to bring the balm of healing peace to an aggravated situation or relationship. When we experience the descent of her presence, we will understand the dynamo that is peace. It is related to the munificence of the creative power that informs silence.

Angel of Peace-Making
Gav-reel

Her mode is usually feminine; she is the Peace-Maker angel, known to many tribes in touch with the spirit of the Earth, especially the Native Americans, who smoked the peace pipe and buried the hatchet in her honour. She is sister to Gabriel, and is an aspect of her soul. As a visionary angel she can be seen with the eyes of the soul, pouring balm onto troubled waters. Her garments are dove-white; her music is continuous song, from slow surging strains to the highest ethereal notes of plaintive sweetness, accompanied by a hushing, lulling sound like soft sea swells; her perfume is a heavenly combination of lavender and rose.

Gavreel resolves situations of enmity and conflict into forgiveness, acceptance and peace. As well as helping us to make peace with our enemies, Gavreel fosters mental and emotional balance and brings the balm of peace to troubled minds. Those enduring destructive stress or otherwise in need of equilibrium can invoke Gavreel and her merciful powers. Call on her in all fraught or dangerous situations. If you cannot love your neighbours, invoke Gavreel to love them for you! Then an inroad to peace will quietly manifest.

The Release of St. Peter, c.1635 (oil on canvas), by Bernardo Strozzi (1581–1644). Art Gallery of New South Wales, Sydney, Australia/The Bridgeman Art Library

Angel of Rain
Yur-a

Her mode is usually feminine; she shimmers with light, and her light dances; her robes often manifest as garments of softly falling rain alive with her dancing lights; their colour is a soft grey, like a wild dove or the first skies of dawn with their promise of muted but clear and lovely light beyond their hushed flanks of shadow; her music is the soft swelling drumbeats, tiny but a million-fold strong, of fulsomely falling rain when it fills the silence of the landscape; her perfume is that of warm rain hydrating the thirsty aromatic earth.

Call on her to enter into the mysticism of rain and understand its vast miracle. The Mandaeans spoke of this angel as 'the great mystic Yura'. She will lead your meditation if you take time to dwell deeply upon the falling rain. It holds within it the secrets of all creation, of its very first moments. Let the secrets of the rain, its incessant giving, water whatever is parched within you. Pragmatically, you can always ask Yura to stop the rain for a while, or to bring it on if there is a drought.

Angel of the Rays of the Sun
Sham-shi-el

His mode is usually masculine; he is named as 'the prince of Paradise'; he manifests as a clear molten-gold flame; his music seems to come from the stars and can only be described as 'star joy'; his perfume is the rose of Paradise, which grows 'at the summit of the celestial garden' and seeds itself to create the 'heart of hearts' within mortals.

There are powers and mysteries in the sun's rays of which few avail themselves. We have the urge to sunbathe, but rarely follow through with what we are truly being guided to do, which is to breathe in the spiritual atoms of the sunlight and call on it for our healing, renewal, strength and revelation. Enter into the process in the calm of silence and, with an act of intention, peacefully breathe the sun's rays into your heart. Do it every day for a few moments. Shamshiel will oversee the process and configure you anew. Will you receive his life-changing gifts?

Angel of Rejuvenation
Af-ri-el

Her mode is usually feminine; she is described as an angel of force, of the supreme power of the heavens; her robes shine forth with a mighty radiance, casting circles of pure light outwards from her heart which encompass and fortify those who call on her. She manifests as a profoundly beautiful black Madonna, bearing a form very much like Isis. At her heart is a six-pointed star which burns with a coruscating intensity of white-silver light. Her eyes are golden pools of incandescent beauty, radiant with the essence of the sublime realm of which her eyes are a manifestation and a portal. Her music is a rapturous yet steady pulsation, like the distant beating of celestial drums. Her perfume is sandalwood and the musk of the dew rising from the pristine earth.

Afriel imparts youth and vitality, and reminds us that old age is actually nothing more than a thought-form to which we sub-scribe. She brings rejuvenation and vigour to our physical and subtle organs and to our jaded, earth-tired psyches. Call on her to drive away the spectre of soul-heavy, stultifying age so that your heart remains eternally young. This exquisite being does indeed emanate divine force, sweeping her wings in rhythmic encircling pulses of love, upliftment and protection. She shields the inner child residing within each one of us, and is a guardian of children and all that is young and growing.

Angel of the Rising Sun
Gaz-ar-di-el

His mode is usually masculine; he is charged with the setting and the rising of the sun, and especially with the dispersion of the sun's rays at dawn.

He resides in the east and appears to inner vision as a great rayed and winged being, like a sunburst. He holds up his hands in the shape of a cup to receive the beneficence of the glorious rising sun, and then pours it onto the earth as a benediction. The emanation from his wings and his aura is a golden liquid light so beautiful that it seems to lift you up and melt you into the heart of the sun. He 'kisses the prayers of supplicants and conveys them to the supernal firmament', according to one ancient text. When you perceive Gazardiel's glory in all its shining magnificence, it is easy to imagine that a kiss given by him would lend spiritual dynamite to the wings of the prayers he takes under his care!

Gazardiel protects children and all young, tender, growing things. When you long to feel the promise of new beginnings, of a tender enfoldment in newfound innocence after experiencing the sense of its loss, or stand in need of forces of renewal, awakening and a rebirth of enlightenment in your life, teach yourself to face the rising sun each morning and invoke the blithe, radiant, tender Gazardiel.

Angel of Rivers
Da-ra

Her mode is usually feminine; she dwells particularly in the bird–life of rivers; her music is in their fluting, poignant notes, and the rhythms of her energy in their strident calls; her robes are the colour of pristine morning mists and the sparkle of the sun on the water; her eyes hold histories of the 'long persons', the rivers, which are under her charge. Her perfume is the fragrance of blue wood smoke rising from the first kindling and the musk of old-fashioned roses.

Call on Dara to clear and purify polluted rivers, and to release your ethereal body to dance with the river spirit, which always moves us on from stagnation, ventures ever outward, and teaches us to delineate the magical story of our lives.

Angel of Running Streams
Na-hal-i-el

His mode is usually masculine; his garments are of bright, flashing silver; his eyes dart and dance; his music is that of bubbling streams, with effervescent laughter and silvery elfin bell peals in its echoes; fairy life leaps and tumbles in his robes; his perfume is akin to peppermint with a dash of lemon-balm, fresh and invigorating.

Call on Nahaliel when you feel that your life and its energies are growing jaded, stifled and stultified. Let his energies course through you and carry you to a place of diversity and sparkle. Chant his name softly throughout the day, thinking of running streams playfully casting off every clinging fragment of your torpor and turgidity. And whenever you might come across a running stream in actuality, play a game with Nahaliel. Make a little boat from a leaf, set twigs sailing on the water, let the laughing water run through your fingers. This angel loves to play; one of his favourite tricks is to splash you – he loves the feeling of surprise it evinces! Yet beyond his childlike frolicking his angelic self holds its own. There is magic and restorative healing in the sudden embrace of the water, and a therapeutic awakening within the slight thrill of shock it imparts.

Angel of Sanctuary
Sar-Ha-Kodesh

His mode is usually masculine; he wears many radiant crowns; the colour of his robes is all-enfolding and golden; he emits poignant tones of music and a perfume similar to sharp, clean, rain-washed lavender.

Invoke this angel in an emergency when you need to find a place of safety, or when your day is not allowing you time for the space and peace that you need, or when you feel a sense of oppression. Sar-Ha-Kodesh can be called upon when encountering difficult, aggressive or intrusive people, or when you feel that you are a stranger in a strange place.

Angel of the Sea
Bi-nah

Her mode is usually feminine; she is a mighty angel, with robes cascading across the horizon as if she filled the sky; her influences are in the lilt of the waves and the rousing wild cries of the sea birds; her colours are the 'blue and green wine' of the sea; her music is a great symphony of boundless dimensions playing within the roar and boom of the breakers; her perfume has in it elements of thyme and the fragrant fruits of the earth – it is the perfume of life, with a wildness and a tang in it, and a bracing brine.

This angel enfolds the secrets of life to her heart, and if we will allow her to similarly enfold us, we will learn them. We can repay her beneficence by offering prayers to her to cleanse and heal the oceans after humankind's ravages of them, and ask her to restore their eco-systems to their pristine condition.

Call on her also for personal renewal, cleansing, invigoration and the spirit of limitlessness. When you are by the sea, let her lift your soul into the rapture of the waves so that it can bathe in the mystery of the ocean.

Angel of Secrets
Z-lar

His mode is usually masculine; he is the profundity beyond the chatter of the clamorous everyday mind, and is one of the company of 'the glorious and benevolent angels of Heaven'; the colour of his robes is silver-touched indigo, like a starry night; his music is the strains of a rolling organ, deep and grave but exquisite in its majesty; his perfume is the smoke of sacrificial fires, burning no sentient creature but rather herbs, grain and honey.

'Ask, and it shall be given; seek, and ye shall find; knock, and the door will open.' When you need spiritual insight and penetrative perception, call on this mighty being, who reveals secret wisdom. Whilst Zlar imparts secrets that we need to know at certain junctures in our lives, he also assists us in appropriately keeping secrets and in guiding us as to when to speak and when to maintain silence about the secrets we enshrine within ourselves.

Angel of Self-Discipline
Mai-on

Her mode is usually feminine; she is set over self-discipline, focus, and concerted and prolonged effort; she teaches us how to persevere. Her robes are a radiantly bright silver-white; her movements are slow and majestic; her music is measured and sonorous; her perfume is that of night-scented stock.

This bright spirit holds up the ideal of wise self-regulation and denial of the demands and dominion of the lower self, but counsels against harshness. She reminds us that self-flagellation can be a form of indulgence! Attune yourself to this angel to learn the gentle but persistent art of self-governance. She will increase your capacity for focus, force of effort and self-discipline.

Angel of Self-Knowing
El-e-miah

His mode is usually masculine; like Cosmiel, he is an angel of voyagers; he blesses maritime feats, but he also presides over the voyages we undertake into the deeps of ourselves. This angel blesses the depths of our self-awareness. His robes are of silver fire; his music is peaceful and beautiful, with the crashing of waves within its dimensions; his perfume is the tang of salt, the brine that you smell and taste on a day full of benign gales and gusts at the seaside.

Call on this radiant one to illuminate blind spots, blinkeredness, and ignorance or distorted ideas of self. Elemiah will also show you the sublime reaches of your inner beauty, and teach you to be humble as a divine dewdrop in the vast rolling ocean of all that is.

Angel of Silence
Cha-roum

Her mode is usually feminine; she wears a crown of supernatural diamonds whose measureless purity is the essence of silence, for silence is the crown of enlightened consciousness. The colour of silence is pure white, pure light, brilliant yet softly shining. Her perfume is the inner essence of the rose.

In the sound of her name is the rhythm of silence. If you create a measured chant from its repetition, softening the 'Ch' to 'Sh' and

The Angel, (oil on panel), by Sir Edward Coley Burne-Jones (1833–98).
Glasgow Museums, UK/© Culture and Sport Glasgow (Museums)/The
Bridgeman Art Library

lingering on the second syllable, the soothing music of her name steals into the soul with a sense of profound hush. The sound of silence is golden, measureless and pure.

Whenever you need the dynamic of peace both within and without, you can summon the blessing of both Charoum and Valohel (see above). Charoum blesses the art of listening and teaches us to set a guard over our tongue. 'There is a mighty power in silence,' say the angels. How often in life do we feel pressured, really against our will, to say something, to respond with some remark, when it would be better not to do so, but rather to keep a gracious silence? Those who can be graciously silent reveal themselves thereby as old initiates. They have mastered the art of silence. Let us remember the option of silence, with all its poise, dignity and peace.

When we enter into the silence, we enter into the deepest point of our creativity and touch the 'nous', the doorway between the soul and the spirit.

Angel Healer of Skin Infections
A-marl-i-a

Her mode is usually feminine; according to ancient texts, she came out of the land of Sodom, a centre of great learning and excellence, to heal painful boils; her robes are pure, cooling water; her eyes are pale golden and soft with compassion; her music is like the high notes of a piano, poignant and sweet with a liquid 'plinking' sound; her perfume is the scent of Melissa.

Call on Amarlia, together with Raphael, the Angel of Healing, to take away distressing skin conditions. Open yourself to the influences of these angels and see them pouring into you like a great riverfall of cleansing light.

Angel of Sleep and Oblivion
Pur-ah

His mode is usually masculine; his wings are a great embrace of hushed peace; he is the soul of stillness and deep lulling spiritual gulfs of calmness and serenity; his robes are the colour of shaded light and an ethereal, pearly grey; his music is dreamy, soft and stealing; his perfume is frankincense, lavender and balm.

Call on Purah and the Angels of Sleep when insomnia strikes. Summon this great Angel of oblivion when it would be better for you to forget something, such as an insult, a worrying situation, a failed love affair or marriage, or a particular person who does not return your affection. Sometimes, you just need to forget your worries for the duration of the night. Purah stands ready to help.

Angel of the Snows
Shal-gi-el

Her guise is usually feminine; the colour of her robes is the bright white purity of diamonds that glints on virgin snow; her music is sweet, like mandolins, but symphonic, moving in swells and slow grandeur; her perfume, like that of Ilaniel, is the fragrance of fresh apples plucked straight from the tree.

Call on Shalgiel to alleviate problems with snow. If it is falling too fast and you are caught out in it either in a vehicle or whilst walking, ask her to lessen it and gentle the snowfall, and to keep you safe until you reach shelter.

If you are trudging through fallen snow, ask her to guard your footsteps and to ease your journey. If it is mounting up outside alarmingly so that your community may be cut off, ask her to bring the snowfall to a stop.

If you are walking in snow, ask her to prevent the snowflakes from stinging and blinding you. Shalgiel loves to convey the magic and wonder of snow to humans. Its chill and inconvenience tend to mask these qualities, but Shalgiel releases a blessing so that the complaints of the body don't obscure the perception of the soul. Invoke Shalgiel to reveal the enchantment and beauty of the snow, the mystical purity and majesty of its spiritual dimension, the way it opens up a door onto other worlds. Revel in the joy of the snow. Children sense that each snowflake is a miracle. Elizabeth Goudge entitled her autobiography *The Joy of the Snow* after hearing a child exclaim 'Look, look at the joy of the snow!'

Angel of Solitude
Cass-i-el

His mode is usually masculine; he 'shows forth the unity of the eternal kingdom'; he breathes the spirit of beauty and the spirit of profundity over the landscape of solitudes, ensouling them and revealing their indwelling divinity; his robes are a soft sanctified purple, like glorious twilight clouds over the ocean; he rides the ascended dragon of Divine Spirit; his eyes are deep indigo, holding midnight's stars; his music moves in slow symphonies of brooding, pensive poignancy lifting to exultation; his perfume is the incense of pine and cedar wood.

Call on Cassiel when you feel poetry stirring in your soul and you need to set your spirit free.

Some time regularly spent in solitude deepens the soul and releases the spirit. Cassiel enfolds us in his protection and ensures that we do not stray into a sad isolation of self.

Angel of the Star of Love
An-a-el

Her mode is usually feminine; she appears in robes of soft blues, turquoise transforming into muted emerald green, and shades of subtle rose, delightfully delicate, like the pink of a conch shell lit by sunlight of such clear lustre that its radiance seems the ineffable light of happiness. Anael serves the planet Venus, which has a special link with the Earth and the Moon. She presides over sexuality and the currents of its correct flow. 'Open all ye gates!' is Anael's cry. The concept of opening and entering is profoundly sacred and protected by Anael as the deepest mystery of eroticism. Her music is a melodious hum produced by choiring voices with impressions of electric forces and powerful vibrations within its resonance; her perfume is the erotic rendition of the rose, which has the name of the god of love, Eros, within it as an anagram.

Anael (sometimes known as Haniel) teaches us to experience romantic love from a standpoint of poise, balance and sanity. Invoke her to guide you in your sexual relationships. Although most of us want wildness, poetry and passion in our deepest love-affairs, these elements have to be kept in creative rather than destructive mode. Their keynote must be love rather than gratification. Anael shows us how to achieve a proper perspective by combining personal love with unconditional love, and unconditional love with the appropriate degree of responsibility to self.

She teaches us to embrace wisdom, insight and stability whilst we enjoy the euphoria of being in love. Anael also blesses love for oneself (again, the correct resonance of it). If feelings of inadequacy and under-confidence present themselves, or uneasiness in social situations rears its head, call on Anael to soothe and heal the fear and disturbance. She will restore you to your true self and empower you to operate from a place of ease within.

Angel of Strength and Endurance
Geb-u-rath-i-el

Geburathiel's mode is often androgynous; this angel sometimes appears as an angelic prince, mounted on horseback, representing 'the divine strength, might and power'. A crown of glory irradiates the aura of Geburathiel; her garments are fiery; his perfume is the fragrance of cypress, both the aromatic oil and the subtle cleanly musk of the leaves after rain.

When you need to invoke the quality of strength, of will, of body, of purpose, strength for the aura or the strength of courage, endurance and resilience, call on Geburathiel, one of the princely chiefs 'set over strength'.

Angel of Tears
San-dal-phon

His mode is usually masculine; he is the great Angel of the Earth and Angel of the Embryo; he is also called the 'bright lord of prayer'; the colour of his robes is a beautiful combination of pastel orange, peach, softly radiant autumn red, russet, amber and clear pale gold; he wears, as his name implies, golden sandals with which he walks upon the earth, although they are symbolically winged, for of course he is not earthbound. He is the gentle master of tears and presides over their flow.

He works with the Angels of Sorrow to comfort, to bring peace and healing to troubled hearts. He understands the sorrows of earth, and although his music can be joyful and celebratory it can also move in deep modes of sorrow. His perfume is the deep, rich, mellow fragrance of autumn, touched with a pure celestial poignancy, as are all the fragrances of the angels.

Call on the Angel of Tears to calm and still your grief. Ask that the Angels of Sorrow draw close to sweeten and soften its resistant core. You will be lifted into a transformative world where your grief no longer ravages you but becomes a wellspring which feeds the roots of your being. You can send this blessing to others who might be grieving, depressed or sorrowful.

Angel of Tidal Rivers
Tir-is-i-el

Her guise is usually feminine; there is a stirring of the air about her, for she carries the frequencies of tidal rivers with all their rushing rapids, rolling currents and roiling undertow. Her robes are blue-silver and willow green. Her presence can be sensed among the rushes and the reeds as well as the river's restless undulating breast. Her music is the liquid strain of harps; her perfume is warm and wide-ranging, with hints of cinnamon and coriander.

Call on Tirisiel to cleanse and reinvigorate polluted tidal rivers, their herbiage, trees and wildlife. You can use Tirisiel's potencies to charge all your prayers and blessings. Write them on undyed bio-degradable paper, twist them into figures of eight (symbol of the continuous life-flow and the frequencies of the Sacred Marriage) and cast them on the waters. Tirisiel, at your request, will charge them with her onflowing energies and bear them to their spiritual destination.

Invoke this revivifying angel when you wish to enter a state of dream and reverie, seeing your life and its purposes and aspirations rolling and surging on to the boundless ocean, expanding their horizons and then setting sail for undreamt-of shores.

Treasure-Finding Angel
Sed-e-kiah

His mode is usually masculine; he exudes feelings of positivity and joviality; his robes are bright and intense, like a spotlight or a fiery beam of golden-white; his music is a soft, growing swell, like a crescendo of encouragement and anticipation; his perfume is that of the sweet pungency of cloves.

Sedekiah teaches us to pounce artfully, with laughter and joy and without avarice, like a cat that has retained its kitten nature. Ask Sedekiah for help when you are seeking something valuable and elusive. His stipulation is that your desire for discovery must accord with right relationships. (If you are on a morally dubious quest, you will not get Sedekiah on side, but a spirit of a very different order!) Sedekiah will bless your treasure hunt with success. He functions on many levels, so, for instance, a poet may net the word required, a home-maker will light on an item at the right price and of the right colour, a lonely person will meet a friend or a romantic partner or some other path out of their isolation, a seeker after knowledge will find a teacher or a book or an intuitive illumination, an ornithologist might be led to the haunt of a rare bird, or a literal treasure-hunt will yield results. Angels are both literal and non-literal in their service to us, so when calling on an angel such as Sedekiah it is of great benefit to try to exceed the limitations of our own thinking!

Sedekiah is also the Angel of Serendipity, which means that on our treasure hunt, be it literal or figurative, we may well discover something of equal or greater value that had never occurred to us as an objective. The realization then dawns that this unexpected find was the deeper cause of the original search.

Angel of Trees
Zuph-las

Zuphlas manifests in androgynous mode and is the great angel protector of trees, who can be called upon to heal and bless individual trees, copses and woodland, or the great forests of the world. We hear the grandeur of Zuphlas's music when the wind is in the treetops, or when we stand and listen, in utter stillness of soul, within the depths of winter or summer woods. His perfume is that of flowering woodbine.

Zuphlas is eager to work with us. Call on this angel when wandering and standing amongst trees in contemplation of them. If you are seeking to bring wisdom and angel blessings to a political assembly which will make decisions about the environment, call on Zuphlas to descend upon and inspire those who will receive her-his guidance.

Angel of Truth
Ar-mai-ta

Her mode is usually feminine; she is spoken of as 'the spirit of truth, wisdom and goodness who became incarnate to help the good-willed among humanity'; the colour of her robes is a glorious magenta; her music is softly symphonic, as if caught on the wind, incorporating also the ancient rhythms of the tabor given forth by dancers; her perfume is that of the flowering earth.

Call on this gracious one when you feel confused and are grasping after clear vision. As the great archangel presiding over truth, wisdom and goodness, she fosters harmonious, balanced, cooperative relationships with others, and will help you in the establishment and healing of these relationships. She will also give tremendous impetus to deeds done in the name of truth, wisdom and goodness. Offer them on her altar before engaging in them; if they pass Armaita's stringent tests, she will bless them indeed. If they fall short, she will reveal the truth behind your or another's motives, but with gentleness and kindness.

Angel of Ultimate Protection
Mi-cha-el

His mode is masculine; with his twin flame Shekinah, Michael heads the angel hosts. His sword is the sword of truth, his white horse is the steed of purity, his shield throws off vivid albescence. He is called 'magnificently radiant', 'a pillar of light', 'Michael the Valiant', 'Brightness of the Mountains', 'Great Chief of the Angels', 'Michael of the white peace', 'sun-radiant one', 'brightest warrior' and 'the embodiment of honour perfected'. Archangel Michael was the original slayer of the dragon (St George is a human expression of his energies), and his awe-inspiring authority sweeps away every shadow and encroachment. His colours are white and gold; his music is the swell of the celestial choirs; his perfume is the fragrance of the white rose.

Call on this great Angel of Ultimate Protection whenever you are in danger from any threat from any source. You can send his protection to others when they are vulnerable. Step into his circle of light and fear no evil.

Angel of Unconditional Love
She-kinah

Her mode is feminine; exalted among angels, consort to Archangel Michael, she is a being of inconceivable fire; Shekinah, 'brighter than all the stars', archangel of grace and rarefied flame with eyes of radiant love, walks in the light of the highest heavens; her robes are the essence of glory; her music is the rapture of celestial halls; her perfume is the breath of the Divine.

When you need to express unconditional love – perhaps at a time of crisis – and you feel yourself struggling, call on Shekinah and bathe in her radiance. You will find utter love, utter strength, utter peace. No darkness can withstand the light of Shekinah. Chant her name and let her unbind your heart and lift you into miracles of love you never thought you could achieve.

Angel of Unveiling
Ith-ur-i-el

His mode is generally masculine; his robes are like clear water irradiated by reflected sunbursts; he works with the Angel of Truth (Armaita) and the Angel of Hidden Things (Satarel) to fulfill his tasks, and stands within the dimensions of a great golden crown glowing beautifully with an outflow of exquisite light, which emphasizes his blessing of the crown chakra and its circle of perception; his music is a very intense, cleansing sound, like silver bells pealing in a sublime and secret place; his perfume is the exudation from fresh pine wood.

Ithuriel lifts the veil of illusion or deception from the face of a person, a situation, an intention, a proposition or a concept. He exposes traps and guile. If we are very brave, we might even dare to ask him to expose our own areas of vacuity and falsity! We can be assured he will bring healing to them rather than blame and chastisement. Call on him when you feel unsure, or even *too* sure, about a certain scenario, situation or predicament – feeling bull-headed about something can be a sign that guile has got to you! Milton depicts Ithuriel in *Paradise Lost* as uncovering the guile of Satan in the Garden of Eden, coming upon the 'grieslie king' disguised in a glamour of illusionary form, 'sqat like a Toad close at the ear of Eve'. On touching the lord of evil with his spear of light, Ithuriel threw off Satan's glamour so that he resumed his true lineaments. Although today people are beginning to reach after a more enlightened interpretation of the symbolic drama in the Garden of Eden, Milton's poetic rendition makes its point about Ithuriel to perfection.

The Voices: Soul-Summoning Angels
(Just chant their name softly to invoke their protection.)

The Gnostics described these enigmatic angels as angelic entities inhabiting the Treasury of Light. From this Treasury they have gifts to bring us, gifts of inner counselling, guidance, enlightenment, comfort and inspiration. When we are weary, getting nowhere, when we seem to have turned blind and deaf to all spiritual direction, when we seem to come up against a brick wall, then we call on The Voices. Tradition tells us there are seven Voices. They have passed into folklore as the Seven Whistlers (birds with a melancholy call, such as plovers, curlews or lapwings, who foretell tragedy, especially on the sea) and the Seven Wish Hounds (baying voices who also foretell death).

It is interesting to note that folklore is full of doom and gloom concerning The Voices, when actually they bring life and hope! Sometimes they do issue a warning, but only with the expectation of averting the threatening incident, not for the pleasure of prophesying woe!

Attune to the wild call of The Voices, pray to them to be with you in times of need, and you will hear them in natural sounds whenever your attention needs to be drawn to something or someone, or perhaps to yourself. Sometimes they bring a warning; sometimes they say, 'Think again'; sometimes they sound a reproach; sometimes they foretell an important event so that you can prepare for it at the subtler levels of life. Always they come as an act of angelic love and protection.

Angel of Voyaging
Cos-mi-el

Her mode is usually feminine; Cosmiel is an angel so magnificent in her freedom that her unfettered voyagings circumnavigate the cosmos; her robes are a trail of stars and fire-mist. A whirlwind of spiced and perfumed breezes moves through her, giving exhilaration and the daring spirit of adventure to the journeyer. As she inspires this intrepid and invincible stance, so she simultaneously enfolds the journeyer in wings as bright and powerfully protective as a wayfarer's moon. Her music is exhilarating, like Vivaldi's high energy outbursts.

Call on Cosmiel when you are undertaking an adventure or a voyage into unknown regions, whether these are of the mind, the soul or the body.

Be brave and let her lead! Cosmiel was the angel who escorted the 17th-century Jesuit Athanasius Kircher on his astounding journeys to other planets. Kircher reports on this 'ecstatic voyage' in his *Oedipus Egyptiacus*.

It is tempting to think that the creator of *Star Trek*, with its protagonist Captain Kirk, was familiar with this intriguing tome!

Angels of Water

These are traditionally known as Azariel, Tharsis, Michael, Gabriel, and Nahaliel. They protect, cleanse and heal all bodies of water on earth. The Angels of Rivers are Tirsiel and Dara. The 'supreme Lord of the Waters' is Phul. See them in robes like cataracts, their waters purling purest white and adorning them in pristine clouds of ether. Their music is the symphony of mighty rapids, their perfume the scent of immaculate cleanliness.

We can invoke their powers and benediction when we want to bring healing to the waters of the earth – a task that the angels will delight in and bless us for. When you wish to enter deeply into the spirit of water, whilst swimming or bathing or enjoying the proximity of a rill or stream, chant the names of the angels of water and free up the emotional energies of your life.

Teach children to connect with the Angels of Water whilst splashing in puddles!

Angel of the Waters of the Soul
Sach-a-el

Her mode is usually feminine; she teaches us what water really is in the higher realms; her music has a high, sweet, silvery tone, like a glockenspiel; it is the sound of bliss. Her perfume is the honeyed heather of high moors in summertime, where mountain tarns reflect the spirit of Sachael; her robes are composed of jewels overlaid by clear water. To receive an inkling of her beauty, place some crystals in a glass vessel and cover them with spring water; the fairyland loveliness of the crystals thus viewed is enthralling. Sachael shows us that the soul itself actually takes its body from an exalted form of ethereal water. She fosters our intuitive powers and brings to us an awareness and understanding of our deepest feelings. She teaches us how to perfectly reflect the still flame of the spirit so that we can claim our highest birthright. She releases pressure and disturbance from the unconscious realms, and makes clear and pure any area of the waters of our soul that have grown murky and unwholesome.

Call on this angel when you are not at peace with yourself, when some inner disquietude cannot be identified, yet persists. It is at these times that we need to listen to the voice of our soul, which speaks and offers guidance first through our feelings before translation into thought. Having learned to give ear to the promptings of the soul, we can continue to listen to that inner voice constantly. Attune to Sachael, to the waters of the soul, and allow her to serve you. You will be absorbed into her transforming light.

Angel of Wild Animals
Mit-ni-el

Her mode is usually feminine; her robes can assume the sacred patterns and colours of the wild beasts she protects, burnished with a rich, haunting gold; on other occasions she is simply a lyrical white presence. Her music, sometimes deep, sometimes high-pitched, is a slow, rapt, note of joy building to a crescendo; her perfume is the scent of the woods in the autumn. Send greetings to her when you walk in woodland, because it is in the woods – in the refined dimensions of the trees – that she makes her home. The spirit of Mitniel can sometimes descend into a wild creature so beautifully and completely that the animal assumes an ethereal angelic form; this transcendent vehicle of light can be seen via sensitive sight within its physical body and has become an expression of its developing soul.

As the guardian angel of wild animals, Mitniel helps us to heal our animal brethren with prayers for their welfare and the preservation of their habitats. She will also help to shine angelic light into the vision of those entrusted with decisions relating to the environment. She performs this task with the charge created by our prayers, although naturally the free will of those on whom she focuses is always respected. Call on Mitniel to beautify, deepen and enrich your understanding of and relationship to our wild animal brethren.

Angel of the Wilderness
Or-if-i-el

His mode is usually masculine; there is a certain cragginess, a strength as of boulders, to Orifiel, and also a pure, sweet, poignant wildness that vibrates through him like the song and the wing-beats of an invisible bird; his robes carry the imprint of mountains with their snow and stone; the mysticism of the desert dwells in his eyes; the expanse of the plain is in his wings; the canopy of the forest breathes through his perfume.

The essence of Orifiel dwells within the human soul, and without the spirit of the wilderness, that collective soul would lose its proper dimensions. Call on Orifiel to help you to connect to nature, for nature is our spiritual as well as our physical source. Call on him to evoke the beautiful spirit of the wilderness in your soul when you are hedged in by buildings, commercial culture and the 'pavement grey', as the poet Yeats invoked the Isle of Innisfree when the city oppressed his senses. When we wish to heal and protect wild places in nature, we summon the stewardship of Orifiel.

Angel of the Winds
Ruh-i-el

His mode is usually masculine; he suspires and weaves over us in life-giving gales; his garments are moving air, billowing about him in flashes and sparkles of muted silver; his music is ethereal and whispering, like pan-pipes; his perfume is exotic, rich and full-bodied.

Summon Ruhiel when you need oxygen on every level. Let him caress your hair and take your breath. He will restore it to you infused with stories and imaginings. Invoke him to blow away the cobwebs, and listen to him moving like a ghostly sighing saurian among the treetops and harrying the clouds into fantastical pictures of the mind.

Angel of Wholeness
Haur-va-tat

Her mode is usually feminine; she is the personification of salvation; Zoroastrianism designates her 'the spirit of the waters' and the essence of wholeness, for her presence is the act and the state of holistic integration and wholesomeness. Haurvatat's presence is overarching, like the grandeur, peace and sanctity of a cathedral. The colours of her robes are the colours of the rainbow and the spectrum's resolution of purest white; her music is the expression of the deep hush over the earth when the peace of profound night falls and we return to the inner worlds; her perfume is a flow of divine rapture, with subtle flower scents exactly as they are when inhaled fresh from the living petals, and a distinct impression of clean linen!

Call on Haurvatat to help you when your inner feeling of wholeness is disrupted, by a person, an injustice, by circumstances or by ill-health. Haurvatat gives her blessing in cases of mental illness, when the body or emotions are thrown off kilter, or when an encounter leaves you feeling as if someone has disturbed, or even stolen or become dominant over, a part of your soul. Haurvatat will restore you to wholeness and take away the feelings of intrusion and uncleanliness.

Angel of the Zenith
John

His mode is usually masculine; he is also known as the Angel of the Pointing Hand. Leonardo has painted him many times, for in his images of him he depicted not the man, but the angel within the man. His robes are rays of the sun; they clothe him like a sun-flare. His music is tremendous, like the pounding of cosmic waves. His perfume is the perfume of a tree both in blossom and in fruit growing at the heart of the orchard of heaven.

The Angel of the Zenith points upward, at the highest pinnacle of achievement. Yet he points also at the heart, into the depths of human perception. Only in the highest consciousness of the heart – the human being in its wholeness – can the pinnacle of achievement be attained. Within his heart, John enshrines a beautiful understanding and love of Divine Mother.

Call on the Angel of the Zenith to help you to surpass your limitations and imbue you with the vision, power and fortitude to realise your highest aspirations.

✳

On completion of any angelic communion, remember to send loving thanks to those you have called upon. This outflow of gratitude will help to open your deeper being to the angels and will create strong vital bonds of friendship, sensitive awareness and joy between you and your shining companions.

✳

Picture Credits

Love and the Maiden, 1877 (tempera with gold paint & gold leaf on canvas), by John Roddam Spencer Stanhope (1829–1908). Private Collection/Photo © Christie's Images/The Bridgeman Art Library

Detail of the Angel, from *The Virgin of the Rocks (The Virgin with the Infant St. John adoring the Infant Christ accompanied by an Angel)*, c.1508 (oil on panel), by Leonardo da Vinci (1452–1519). National Gallery, London, UK/The Bridgeman Art Library

Raphael and Tobias, 1507–8 (oil on panel), by Tiziano Vecelli Titian (c.1488–1576). Galleria dell' Accademia, Venice, Italy/The Bridgeman Art Library

Cupid and Psyche, (oil on canvas), by Sir Edward Coley Burne-Jones (1833–98). Sheffield Galleries and Museums Trust, UK/Photo © Museums Sheffield/The Bridgeman Art Library

The Release of St. Peter, c.1635 (oil on canvas), by Bernardo Strozzi (1581–1644). Art Gallery of New South Wales, Sydney, Australia/The Bridgeman Art Library

The Angel, (oil on panel), by Sir Edward Coley Burne-Jones (1833–98). Glasgow Museums, UK/© Culture and Sport Glasgow (Museums)/The Bridgeman Art Library

An Angel, 1525 (fresco), by Bernardino Luini (c.1480–1532). Sanctuary of the Blessed Virgin of Miracles, Saronno, Italy/The Bridgeman Art Library

Annunciatory Angel, 1450–55 (gold leaf and tempera on wood panel), by Fra Angelico (Guido di Pietro) (c.1387–1455). Detroit Institute of Arts, USA/Bequest of Eleanor Clay Ford/The Bridgeman Art Library

Death of a Butterfly, c.1905–10 (oil on canvas), by Evelyn De Morgan (1855–1919). © The De Morgan Centre, London/The Bridgeman Art Library

Tobias and the Angel, 15th century (oil on panel), by Altobello Meloni (fl.1497–1517). Ashmolean Museum, University of Oxford, UK/The Bridgeman Art Library